We Wuz Robbed!

WE WUZ ROBBED!

Bud Greenspan

GROSSET & DUNLAP
Publishers · New York
A Filmways Company

I'd probably still be writing this book
if Nancy Beffa hadn't showed up one day.

Photographs courtesy of:

United Press International: 20 (right), 21, 23, 24, 25, 55, 56,
    57, 65 (bottom), 66—67, 68 (top, bottom), 69, 71, 72,
    75, 76, 77, 78, 79, 80 (center, bottom), 81, 84, 85,
    86—87, 88, 89, 90, 91, 95, 97 (bottom), 98—99, 100,
    106, 107, 110, 111, 112, 113, 124, 125, 127, 129,
    130—31, 134, 135, 136, 137, 142, 143, 148, 155, 158,
    159, 181, 183, 184, 186, 187.

Wide World: 27 (top), 47, 49, 50 (top, bottom), 51, 52 (top,
    bottom), 83, 97 (top), 126, 141, 161, 164, 168 (left),
    169 (right, far right), 185.

New York Racing Association: 165.

Published simultaneously in Canada

Library of Congress catalog card number: 74-27946
ISBN 0-448-11855-6 (hardcover)
        0-448-12456-4 (paperback)

First printing

Printed in the United States of America

". . . ask not for victory, ask for courage. For if you can endure you bring honor to us all, even more, you bring honor to yourself."

From *The Deacatlon*

To Cappy, who endured.

Contents

Introduction

IF ALL THE PEOPLE WHO CLAIMED TO HAVE BEEN
eyewitnesses to Bobby Thomson's monumental home run
that won the pennant for the New York Giants over the Brook-
lyn Dodgers on October 3, 1951, at the Polo Grounds were
actually there, more than 100,000 people would have been in
attendance. The fact that the 60,000-seat Polo Grounds was a
little more than half full at that moment does nothing to reduce
the claims of the many who proudly exclaim, "I was there."
Great dramatic sports events go through phenomenal changes
in their retelling.

Jocks who were not born until the 1930s are convinced
that they were at ringside during the Dempsey-Tunney "long
count" bout held in 1927. Baseball buffs of the post–World
War II era speak fondly of the day when Babe Ruth pointed to
the centerfield bleachers before he hit his 1932 World Series
home run. Thirty-year-old tennis devotees recount enthusiasti-
cally that the finest tennis player they've ever seen was Don
Budge, who won his last championship a few years before
World War II began.

Perhaps the most fascinating response to my first book,
Play It Again, Bud, published a few years ago, was the varia-
tion of the same theme: "Thanks for finally setting the record
straight." My second book is the direct result of the readers'
response to *Play It Again, Bud.*

Invariably, the reader would ask, "Why did you leave out the Russian-American 1972 Olympic basketball final?" or "Did the Germans really score in the World Cup final against England in 1966?" or "What happened when Rocky Marciano killed Carmine Vingo in their brutal fight?" The more letters I received requesting a particular event, the more I became interested in making the attempt to find out what really happened.

We Wuz Robbed! is the end result of viewing hundreds of hours of historic films and photographs and reading newspaper stories of the actual coverage of the event by reporters who were there.

I slowed down to frame-by-frame action the moments of controversy, then blew the frames up into still photographs. By this method I was able to view the story in the "present tense" rather than make use of the versions that have become "fact" through years of embellishments.

● It was interesting to read that soccer's famous controversy between Germany and England in the 1966 World Cup Championship was given a one-line mention by the eyewitness reporter. It remains the greatest controversy in soccer history.

● Tom McMillen was one of the U.S. players on the court in the 1972 Olympic basketball final between the Soviet Union and the United States. During our conversations I found it fascinating that he didn't know "what actually happened" until I showed him frame-by-frame frozen action of the final three seconds of the game.

● When I spoke to Tom Hamilton, coach of the Navy football team of 1946, he was firmly convinced that his Midshipmen had lost the final game of the season 21 – 18 to Army because the referee had failed to stop the clock when his player ran out of bounds. The frame-by-frame replay shows conclusively that the referee's decision was correct.

● Congressman Ralph Metcalfe revealed to me some new facts about his controversial losses in both the 100- and 200-meter finals at the 1932 Los Angeles Olympic Games.

● Jockey Ralph Neves was firmly convinced for almost forty years that his horse was in the lead preceding his near-fatal accident at the Bay Meadows Race Track in California. Actually Neves was in fifth place.

We Wuz Robbed! clears up many controversies. Some of the greatest events in sports history are put into sharp focus of what really happened—at the time it happened.

1.
The United States Basketball Team Was Robbed

THE UNITED STATES OLYMPIC BASKETBALL TEAM was cheated out of the gold medal at the 1972 Munich Olympics.

To this day, there is still confusion as to what happened the night of September 9–10, 1972, when the USSR defeated the United States 51–50 to win the Munich Olympics basketball championship. The victory broke a 63-game U.S. winning streak that began at the 1936 Berlin Olympics, when basketball was introduced as an Olympic event.

The replaying of the videotape, and the sworn affidavits of the game officials, document the worst miscarriage of justice in the history of the Olympic Games. The final decision, handed down on January 18, 1973, by the International Olympic Committee, upholding the findings of the Jury of Appeals, dooms for all time the possibility that the United States might receive the reward it rightfully won.

The dramatic final was set up in textbook fashion. The United States went through the preliminary round robin of its division with seven straight victories. Only Brazil gave the Americans any concern. The United States had to come from behind in the final minutes for a 61–54 victory. Meanwhile, in the other division, the Soviet Union went through its seven-game series with nary a scare, winning each contest handily.

The United States swamped Italy 68–38 in the semifinal, but the Russian team had its hands full against Cuba before

With thirty-eight seconds left to go in the game, the Soviet Union leads the United States 49–48.

finally winning 67–61. Since the United States had beaten Cuba by nineteen points earlier, and Russia was all but run off the court by the speedy Cubans in the semifinal before eking out a win, the experts predicted an easy victory for the Americans in the final.

When nine Israeli athletes were murdered in the Olympic Village, the Games were suspended for one day. So the basketball final, originally scheduled for Friday night, was played instead on Saturday, September 9.

Two years before, when the American Broadcasting Company purchased the television rights to the Munich Games, an agreement was reached between ABC-TV, the International Olympic Committee, and the Munich Organizing Committee to hold the basketball final at 11:30 P.M. Munich time so that the game could be seen live in the United States during the late afternoon and early evening hours. Although the game was finished at approximately 8:15 P.M. New York time on the evening of September 9, with the five-hour time difference between New York and Munich, it was the wee hours of the morning of September 10 in Munich when Alexander Belov of the Soviet Union put in the two-pointer that gave the Russians a 51–50 victory.

12

The Soviet Union led at half-time 26–21 as the high-scoring United States team, coached by sixty-eight-year-old Hank Iba, reverted to a 1940s-type of basketball that played right into the Russian's hands. Iba, who hadn't coached college ball for almost ten years, was nevertheless the official United States coach in Tokyo, Mexico City, and Munich. Before the Munich Games, Iba's selection as coach was criticized in many circles. To the critics, Iba's brand of basketball was outmoded when compared to the modern, fast breaking attacks.

With ten minutes to play in the game, the Russians led 38–28. The United States changed tactics and began an all-court press. With little more than six minutes left to play, the Russians still led by eight points, but it was obvious to everyone that the United States was coming on with its more familiar fast-break tactics.

The Russians hung in. They were unable to score a field goal in the last seven minutes of regulation time; nevertheless, they held a 49–48 lead as the clock ran out. With six seconds to go, Doug Collins of the United States picked up a loose ball at mid-court and drove for the basket. He missed the lay-up

After stealing a pass, Collins dribbles downcourt and is fouled as he goes up for his shot. He is awarded two free throws.

but was fouled in the act of shooting. The official clock showed exactly three seconds left in the game.

What followed was the Olympic version of a three-ring circus. Only after screening and rescreening the videotape of the game, and reading the sworn affidavits of the officials, was I able to place in proper order the events that ended in the worst robbery in Olympic history.

With three seconds left to play, Doug Collins picked himself off the floor and walked to the foul line for his two free throws. The score was USSR 49, United States 48. At this point, it is important to clarify the International Amateur Basketball Federation's rules, as opposed to the regulations used in United States collegiate and professional basketball. Three important rules join together as evidence that the United States team was illegally defeated. They are:

> *Article 16: Officials and Their Duties.* The Officials shall be a Referee and an Umpire who shall be assisted by a Timekeeper, a Scorer and a 30-second Operator. . . . The Officials have no authority to agree to changes in the Rules.
> *Article 37: Ball Is in Play:* . . . (b) When the Official places it at the disposal of the free thrower.
> *Article 41: Charged Time-Outs.* A Coach has the right to request a charged time-out. He shall do so by going in person to the Scorer and asking clearly for a "time-out," making the proper conventional sign with his hands. Electrical devices, enabling Coaches to request a time-out without leaving their places, may be used. The Scorer shall indicate to the Officials that a request for charged time-out has been made by sounding his signal *as soon as the ball is dead* and the game watch is stopped *but before the ball is again in play.* (Emphasis mine—Author.)

At the Munich Olympic Games, an electronic buzzer system was used to request a time-out. Each coach had in front of him a button; when pressed, this connected directly to the scorer's table. A time-out could be requested only *when the ball was dead.*

Doug Collins sank his first free throw, and the score was tied 49−49. It will be seen later that at this point the United States lost the game when the International Olympic Committee contradicted its own rules. After Collins sank his first free throw, one of the officials grabbed the ball and tossed it back to Collins, who was standing at the free-throw line. Article 37 clearly states that the ball is in play "when the official places it at the disposal of the free thrower."

Collins sinks his first free throw.

The score is tied 49–49.   **15**

The referee hands the ball to Collins for his second free throw. As soon as a ball is received, international basketball rules prohibit the calling of a time-out. As Collins got ready to shoot, the Russians signaled for a time-out, but the referee rightfully ignored the buzzer.

Collins makes his second free throw.

The United States leads 50–49 with three seconds left in the game.

17

The Russians take the ball downcourt but there is confusion. The referee calls a time-out with one second to play.

Article 41 also clearly states: "A coach has the right to request a charged time-out . . . *as soon as the ball is dead* and the game watch is stopped *but before the ball is again in play.*" (Emphasis mine—Author.) When Collins received the ball from the official, *the ball automatically became in play, and no time-out could be requested.* As Collins got ready to shoot his second free throw, a buzzer sounded. It was ignored by the officials and the players, since a time-out could not be legally called.

Collins made the free throw, and the United States was in front 50—49.

The clock still showed three seconds to play. This was so because even though "the ball is in play" during the actual shooting of a foul, the game clock is stopped.

As Alexander Belov, the 20-point game high scorer for the Russians, took the ball downcourt, the clock was started again. Now Russian officials were converging on the scorer's table. Referee Renato Righetto of Brazil blew his whistle, believing the Russian officials were blocking the view from the scorer's table. Two seconds had elapsed, and the official clock showed one second left to play.

Here is when the illegal act took place. As Referee Righetto rushed to the scorer's table, he was joined by R. William Jones of Great Britain, secretary general of the FIBA and chairman of the Technical Committee for the Olympic basketball tournament. Dr. Jones held up three fingers, signifying that there were three seconds left to play, not one second. He then ordered the clock reset to show three seconds. Dr. Jones acted illegally. He had no official capacity in the orderly running of the game.

Before the clock could be reset to three seconds, play was resumed. After taking the inbound pass, Modestas Paulauskas of the Soviet Union tossed a desperation shot toward the basket: It missed. The United States seemingly had won 50—49.

The United States team and its supporters were hysterical with joy. But the happiness was short-lived. It was apparent that a major discussion was taking place at the scorer's table between Dr. Jones, Referee Righetto, and the scorers and timers. Dr. Jones insisted that play was resumed "illegally" at one second after he had ordered it reset to three seconds. After several minutes of dispute, the clock was reset to three seconds, and the Soviet Union prepared to resume play by tossing the ball from under their own basket. Alexander Belov, the 6-foot 8-inch forward of the Soviets, placed himself

The referee explains to Hank
Iba, coach for the United States
team, that the clock will be reset
to show three seconds to play.

The Russians take a wild shot and miss.
The buzzer sounds for the end of the
game. The United States team is jubilant.

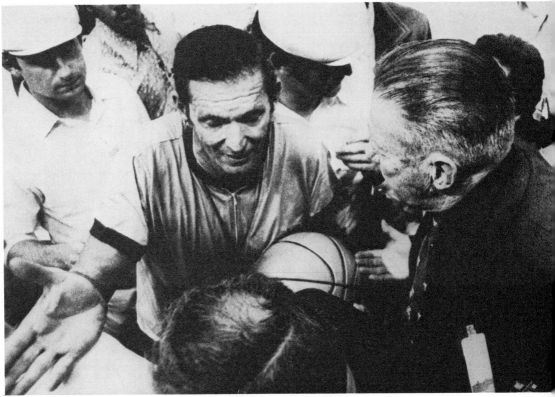

Another meeting is held. The referee explains to Coach Iba that
the Russians did not have a full three seconds to put the ball in
play because the clock had not been set back.

downcourt a few feet from the United States basket. It was obvious to everyone that the Russians would try a desperate full-length court pass to him, with the hope that he, in some way, could catch the ball and shoot it in before time expired. Kevin Joyce and James Forbes of the United States took defensive positions surrounding Belov. Tom McMillen of the United States was the player assigned to guard against the inbound pass.

Inexplicably, McMillen moved several feet back from the end line, giving the Russian an unobstructed alleyway in which to make his desperation full-court pass. The only defense against this particular in-bound pass would have been for McMillen to station himself directly in front of the Russian, arms waving, in order to intimidate the offensive player and obstruct his view. Afterward, McMillen said the referee ordered him away from the end line, giving the Russian a clear pass. The videotape replay clearly shows that the Russian was able to throw his court-length pass undefended.

The pass was perfect. Joyce and Forbes of the United States and Belov of the Soviet Union all went for the ball. Joyce missed his dive, and Belov clearly outmuscled Forbes. The American fell to the floor in what many believe to have been an obvious foul by the Russian, Belov. With both Americans out of the play, Belov easily sank the ball and the Russians led 51–50, when the clock expired for the second time.

The Russians now went through the jubilation scene that the Americans had gone through minutes before. Meanwhile, United States officials stormed the scorer's table, protesting Dr. Jones' illegal and arbitrary decision.

The American protest was first heard by the FIBA Technical Committee and then by a specially appointed jury made up of representatives of Hungary, Italy, Puerto Rico, and Cuba. Here is their official report, based primarily on Dr. Jones' statement:

1. During the execution of the last free throw by the American team and during the last three seconds following it before the end of the playing time, there arose disturbing effects and misunderstandings which influenced the normal flow of play:

The Russians are given a third chance to put the ball in play. Alexander Belov leaps between the two United States defenders. He scores. Russia leads 51–50 as the final buzzer sounds again.

Now the Russians celebrate their victory.

(a) The table signal sounded for time-out during the last free throw which was successful. [Author's note: The sounding of the buzzer was illegal.]

(b) The umpire then started the game; shortly afterwards, the referee signaled to stop the game. Upon this action the game watch was stopped one second before the end of playing time.

(c) Then, upon order of the referee and of the FIBA technical delegate, the table announced that there were three seconds to be played. [Author's note: Read subsequent sworn testimony of game officials.]

(d) The play was, however, resumed without having readjusted the game watch to three seconds to play; consequently, the end signal sounded not after three seconds but one second.

2. After having reset the game watch correctly, during which time the last three seconds were played, the Soviet team scored a valid goal.

The Russian victory was upheld. The United States had one opportunity left; they appealed to the International Olympic Committee in Lausanne, Switzerland, on January 18,

1973, with an impressive array of sworn affidavits from the officials involved, including a statement by Dr. Jones.

The letter written to Lord Killanin, president of the ICC, contained the following sworn testimony of the men at the official scorer's table:

September 16, 1972   SWORN JOINT STATEMENT OF:

Klaus Meyer, Co-ordinator
Horst Baumert, Timer
Manfred Meiser, 30-second Timer
Hans J. Tenschert, Scorekeeper

. . . After the ball was put into play by the Soviets after the second free throw, Referee Righetto interrupted the game and was standing on the side of the court opposite the scoring table. He took a "referee's time-out" since he saw team officials of both the Soviet and American teams coming toward the scoring table from their benches and were blocking the view. Although they did not obstruct our view of the game, evidently Referee Righetto thought they did. Righetto came running across the court toward the Scorer's Table and at the same time Dr. Jones came from the rear to the Scorer's Table and held up three fingers to signal that there

The United States team.

were still three seconds to be played in the game. Then Dr. Jones gave the order to the Longines' technicians to reset the clock to three seconds. *We want to emphasize clearly again that the order to reset the clock was given neither by the Referee nor by the Official's Table, but only by Dr. Jones.*

... Because we do not agree with the points 1-c and 1-d of the Argumentation and Supplementary remarks of the official communique of FIBA which do not correspond with the facts, we see ourselves compelled to clearly describe the last three seconds of the game. ... (Emphasis mine—Author.)

The following sworn testimony taken on September 17, 1972, from Andre Chopard confirms the irregularity of Dr. Jones' action:

I, the undersigned, Andre Chopard, engineer in the service of Longines time-keeping department and technician responsible for the operation of the basketball installation at the Games of the 20th Olympiad in Munich 1972, make the following statement:

At the end of the USSR–USA match, decisive for the first place in the Olympic tournament, Mr. Bigot, the technical representative of the FIBA for this match, asked me, at the request of Dr. Jones, to set back the clock three seconds, although the clock indicated only one second.

In view of the fact that Longines does its work in the service of the organization of the FIBA, I complied with this order in good faith, since it was given to me by the FIBA representative with the support of Dr. Jones.

I would like to add that it is 12-years that I have been time-keeping for Longines and never once in my career as time-keeper at basketball, did anyone ask me to extend the time. ...

The clincher was the sworn statement from Renato Righetto of Brazil, the referee of the game. In his affidavit of November 10, 1972, he said in part:

Paragraph 6

... I was surprised and I didn't know the reason why the general co-ordinator of the controlling table was insisting on the return of the stop-watch [to three seconds]. ... The return of the stop-watch was done by technicians of Longines, with the authority granted to them by the general co-ordinator of the controlling table *and through the intervention of thirds.* ...[The "intervention of thirds" was Dr. Jones.] (Emphasis mine—Author.)

The awards ceremony. The United States declined to appear, stating that it did not wish to jeopardize its appeal by accepting the silver medal. (The Cuban team, at right, receiving bronze.)

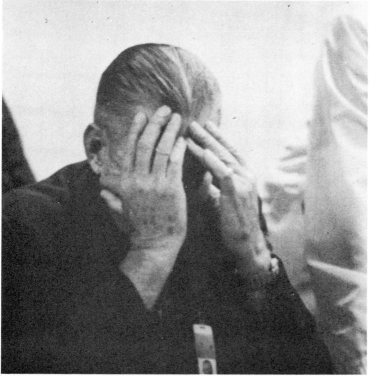

Coach Hank Iba of the United States at a press conference later.

Paragraph 8

    . . . I consider what happened as completely illegal and an infraction to the Rules of Basketball. . . .

The documentation makes it perfectly clear that Dr. Jones usurped his authority and illegally made a decision reserved exclusively for the officials working the game. Nevertheless, the American protest was rejected by the International Olympic Committee, and the Russian victory remains.

As a climax to the messy affair, the game films and videotape replay clearly show two additional oversights by the officials in the final three seconds, either of which would have changed the result. The replay shows that the Soviet player stepped on the end line as he threw his full-court pass to Belov for the final Soviet score. This is a clear violation, and the ball should have been given over to the Americans. The second oversight was equally flagrant. The officials completely missed the fact that Belov stationed himself inside the "three-second lane" for at least five seconds. The officials, in the confusion, evidently forgot that under international rules the three-second rule goes into effect once the official gives the ball to the player out of bounds . . . not when the clock begins.

2.
The Day
Ralph
Neves
"Died"

THE CROWD WAS SILENT. BINOCULARS THAT, SEC-
onds before, had been trained on thoroughbreds pounding
down the backstretch were now focused on a terrible accident
at the first turn. A combination of five horses and their jockeys
were strewn every which way at the bend. Six other horses
had bypassed the muddle and were continuing the race, seemingly unaware of the terrible scene.

Two doctors, who moments earlier had been spectators in
the stands, knelt helplessly over the lifeless form of a jockey
who was spread-eagled and pinned under his dying horse.

The animal's spine had been broken in the fall, and he
was now a dead weight. The doctors, losing precious life-
preserving seconds, could see only the boots of the jockey.
They feared that, if he wasn't already dead, he certainly would
soon suffocate.

Finally, two uninjured jockeys took matters into their own
hands. If the circumstances had not been so tragic, the picture
would have seemed almost comical. It was like a scene out of a
slapstick comedy routine—two small jockeys trying to tug a
horse off the body of their friend. Finally, a third man began
pushing the horse's rump. The combined effort worked. The
injured jockey was freed.

The off-duty doctors had no medical equipment with
them. They quickly felt for life signs, then frantically looked for
help as they realized the condition of the jockey.

Finally, the track ambulance arrived. The official racetrack physician dashed from the rear doors even before the vehicle fully stopped. He, too, felt for life signs. He took his stethoscope from his bag and listened. There was no heartbeat, no pulse. He consulted with the other two doctors, who nodded. They confirmed what he already knew. The jockey was dead.

Twenty thousand spectators watched in shock as the jockey was wrapped in a white sheet. The fans strained to see whether the sheet had covered the jockey's head. Finally, they, too, would know the tragic news as the loudspeaker announced: "Ladies and gentlemen, we regret to tell you that as a result of the accident, jockey Ralph Neves is dead. Will you please stand in silent prayer."

The men in the stands removed their hats. Women were weeping. Many bent on one knee in prayer. Jockeys walked aimlessly in twos and threes. The ambulance drove off.

"Jesus . . ." Ralph Neves whispered. The lights went on, and the motion-picture projector was shut off. "All the stories about what happened were wrong. I've been telling the wrong story for years."

Of course, Ralph Neves is not dead. Today, in his late fifties, Neves is calm and tranquil. He still maintains his jockey weight and has the appearance of a man in his mid-thirties.

The scene was the Talk of the Town restaurant close to the Santa Anita Racetrack in Arcadia, California. The restaurant has made Neves a wealthy man, but as he watched the eerie slow-motion frozen-frame films of the terrible accident, his financial security was of no value. He had just relived those agonizing seconds that preceded his "death" on May 8, 1936. Now, more than forty years later, Ralph Neves had finally found out how it happened.

When he was riding in the 1930s and '40s, they called him "Pepperpot," a comparatively mild nickname for someone who set out to break world records in the number of suspensions he piled up and the carloads of girls he left brokenhearted along the racing trail. The fact that he was the fifth leading American rider when he retired, with more than three thousand victories to his credit, attests to the fact that Neves could find the winner's circle whenever he got down to business.

But that day in May of 1936 he was "dead," and his resurrection is one of the most bizarre stories of American sports.

The day of the accident, Neves was in a four-way fight for

Ralph Neves (arrow), aboard Flanakins, is third from last a split second before the front horse (second from left) is about to trip.

The moment of the accident. Flanakins (arrow) is the back point of a triangle of six horses fighting for the lead.

31

Neves (arrow) appears to have an opening to avoid the accident. But he has already committed Flanakins to move in toward the rail.

the leading-jockey title at Bay Meadows in San Mateo, California, along with Johnny Longden, Jackie Westrope, and Johnny Adams. There were two days to go in the season, and Neves was after the $500 bonus that went to the meet's leading rider.

In the fourth race Neves was aboard Flanakins, third favorite in the betting. The newspaper account the following day described what happened:

> Flanakins broke third, quickly moved up and was first into the backstretch turn. Suddenly he tripped and went down. Neves, hurled straight forward into the rail, bounded off and was ground into the dirt by not one, but four horses running directly behind. . . .

Neves has been telling this newspaper version of what happened for forty years. It was only after I had taken the film he had given me—a scratched, badly lighted print taken from the official patrol-judge footage—and regenerated it into slow-motion frozen-frame images, which made it a perfect modern-day "isolated camera instant replay," that Ralph found out what really happened.

At one time during the screening Ralph whispered: "Jesus—all these years I thought I was in front. I was nowhere near the lead."

The films clearly show that Flanakins broke well, and as they moved into the first turn, Neves was fifth, behind four horses that were stretched from the rail almost to the middle of the track. The frame-by-frame replay shows that the outside horse of the front runners stumbled and bounced into the horse alongside him. Then, in a domino sequence, the other lead horses were hit, and all four went down.

Jockeys were flying through the air as Neves, a few lengths behind, quickly tried to veer around the outside and avoid the crash. The sudden move by Neves evidently confused Flanakins, for he balked. Neves went flying forward over Flanakins' head and several yards forward of the crash. He was evidently stunned and lay stretched out, facing skyward. Incredibly, Flanakins rolled over twice and came to rest directly atop Neves.

The whole sequence took three seconds—seventy-two frames of stop-action slow-motion film.

Looking at the film, Neves almost screamed: "My horse didn't trip. I never hit the rail—I was thrown clear and that damned horse rolled right on top of me. . . ."

33

Neves and Flanakins (arrow)
approach the pile-up.

After the doctors had pronounced Neves dead, the most amazing part of the story took place. Wrapped in a white sheet that covered him from head to toe, Neves was taken to nearby Mills Memorial Hospital where he was placed on a slab in the "cold" room. He would remain there while the death certification papers were filled out, then he would be sent to the morgue.

Neves was stretched out in the "cold" room in total darkness. "All I know is that I leaped up but I couldn't see anything. It was pitch black. I began feeling my way around the room . . . then I started screaming. No one heard me."

The moment of impact.

About thirty minutes had elapsed since he was pronounced dead.

"Finally I found the door and ran like hell. When I got to the street I hailed a cabbie and told him to take me to the racetrack. That cabbie must have thought I was crazy. There I was, wearing only my boots and a sheet."

When the cab arrived at the track, Neves ran out. He didn't have any money, but the cabbie was too scared to force the issue.

Says Neves: "I took one look at him as I dashed out of the door, and he just wanted to get the hell out of there."

35

Neves flying over
Flanakins' head (arrow).

36

Flanakins (bottom) lands on top of Neves (arrow).

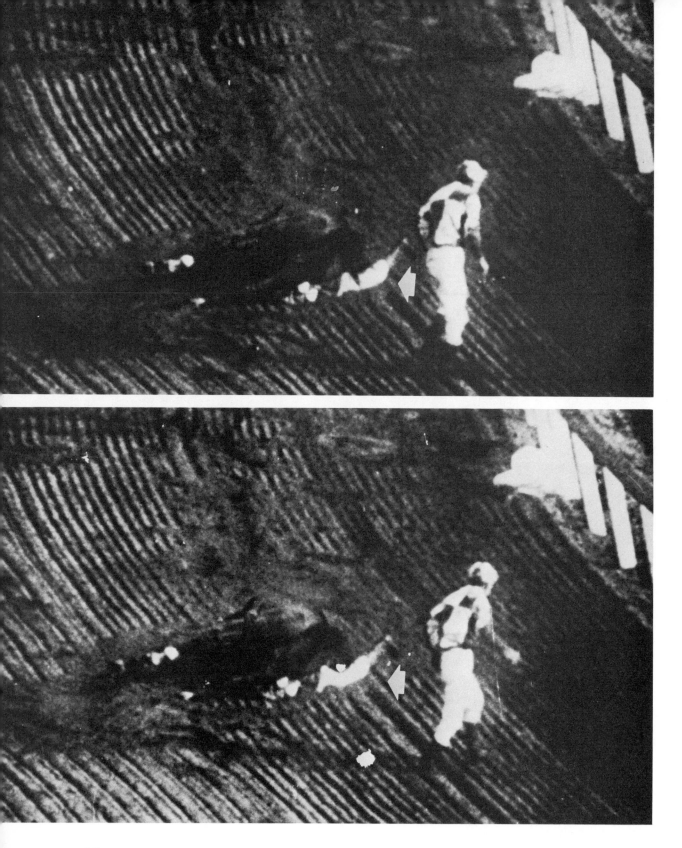

Neves got to the track while several thousand fans were still milling around discussing the tragedy. He began running, and several people started chasing him. Finally, a couple of jockeys caught him and took him back to the track's first-aid station.

He was examined again and, incredibly, this time the doctors could find nothing wrong with him. Except for some bad bruises and a slight case of shock, Neves was pronounced in perfect health.

"Well, you blew the five hundred dollars for the leading jockey title," I said, smiling.

"Are you kidding?" He laughed.

He took me over to a side wall of the lounge and showed me two reprints from the *San Mateo Times* that were not too prominently placed on the wall. One headline read:

RALPH NEVES DECLARED "DEAD." RIDES TODAY.

The other, dated the following day, read:

RALPH NEVES TOP RIDER AT BAY MEADOWS AS MEETING CLOSES.

Another fallen jockey rushes to safety as Neves is pinned underneath Flanakins (arrow).

Bystanders and jockeys tugging
Flanakins off Neves (arrow).

The mortally injured Flanakins is raised
as Neves' legs emerge.

Neves is dragged from underneath
Flanakins. A few minutes later
Neves is pronounced dead.

42

3. Pro Football Dilemma

FAMOUS HORSE-RACE ANNOUNCER CLEM McCAR-thy said sadly a few months before he died, "I've called over a thousand races in my career and the only one I'll be remembered for is the one I called wrong." McCarthy was referring to his description of the Preakness of 1947. He called Jet Pilot the winner, only to realize almost immediately that Faultless was first across the finish line.

McCarthy's epitaph as "the man who called the wrong winner of the Preakness" was the forerunner of a deluge of abuse that is almost weekly voiced by fan, player, coach, and sports executive since videotape and instant replay have put officials on the line because of their controversial decisions. In recent years, officiating in professional football has created the greatest furor.

Perhaps the most famous controversy took place in the 1972 semifinal American Football Conference playoff game between the Pittsburgh Steelers and the Oakland Raiders at Three Rivers Stadium in Pittsburgh. Pittsburgh had the ball on its own 30-yard line and was trailing Oakland 7—6 in the last minute of the game.

With time running out, Steeler quarterback Terry Bradshaw faded back, looking for his flanker, Barry Pearson. Pearson was covered, but Bradshaw spotted halfback Frenchy Fuqua on the Oakland 35-yard line and let loose a desperation pass.

Oakland safety man Jack Tatum and Fuqua leaped for the ball simultaneously. Neither one caught it. The ball was seen to arch some eight yards backward into the hands of Pittsburgh's Franco Harris who galloped 42 yards into the end zone for a touchdown.

The players and spectators were stunned. Referee Fred Swearington, even though Harris was in the end zone, didn't raise his arms in the traditional touchdown signal.

Because contact between Fuqua, Tatum, and the ball took only an infinitesimal part of a second, the legality of Harris's final reception was in question. If Fuqua was the last man to touch the ball before it rebounded to his teammate, Harris, the catch was illegal. Two receivers from the same team cannot touch the ball consecutively. If Oakland's Tatum was the last man to have made contact with the ball, then Harris's reception was legal.

Referee Swearington was in a quandary. He consulted the umpire and back judge for a ruling. After conferring with the other officials, Referee Swearington was confirmed in his own thoughts that the play was legal and that Pittsburgh had scored a touchdown.

However, he placed a call to the press box to consult Art McNally, Supervisor of NFL officials, who was in attendance and had viewed the play several times on instant replay.

McNally asked, "How do you rule?"

"Touchdown," answered Swearington.

McNally replied, "That's right."

Swearington then raised his arms, and the Steelers and their fans knew that the ball game was theirs.

Afterward, the league's executive director, Jim Kensil, denied that McNally's press-box review of the play on videotape had anything to do with Swearington's decision. The answer will never be known since McNally and Swearington agreed on the outcome. There is much speculation as to what might have occurred if McNally, because of instant replay, had told Swearington, "I've seen this play on replay five times and there's no question Fuqua of Pittsburgh was the last man to touch the ball before it bounded back to his teammate Franco Harris." The fact that McNally confirmed Swearington's decision put off, for a time at least, the cry that instant-replay machines be consulted before controversial decisions are made.

Three times during the 1975 professional football season the question of instant replay made headlines.

Sequence photos show the most controversial play in football playoff history.

Frenchy Fuqua of the Pittsburgh Steelers (in black) and Jack Tatum of the Oakland Raiders (in white) both leap for Terry Bradshaw's pass. If the ball had been touched by Fuqua last, what followed would have been illegal.

A collision between Fuqua and Tatum takes place. The ball flies backward. Franco Harris of Pittsburgh (partly hidden by Jack Tatum) snatches the ball before it hits the ground and starts off for a touchdown run.

An unobstructed view of Harris as he reaches for the ball.

The most controversial play of the 1975 football season. Mel Gray of the St. Louis Cardinals apparently has caught the pass as Pat Fischer of the Washington Redskins prepares to crash into him.

On the ninth Sunday of the '75 season, the Eastern Division of the National Football Conference found the Washington Redskins and the St. Louis Cardinals, with identical records of 6 wins and 2 losses, playing against each other. With twenty seconds left to go in the game, the Cardinals trailed Washington by one touchdown.

With the ball on the Redskin 20, St. Louis quarterback Jim Hart spotted his wide receiver Mel Gray slanting across the middle and fired a perfect strike to him at the goal line. Gray seemed to have possession of the ball for an instant, then it was jarred loose by Redskin free safety Pat Fischer as Gray fell to the ground in the end zone. The catch and fumble happened so quickly, it again became one of those subjective calls that could have gone either way.

Referee Fred Silva conferred with the other officials and when the conference broke up, he raised his arms in the touchdown signal. The extra point was made, and the game went into overtime. St. Louis went on to win the game with a field goal. Washington for all practical purposes was knocked out of any playoff consideration, even though the season still had several more weeks to run.

49

Gray is over the goal line but the ball has popped out of his grasp.

The problems of instant replay. The same play from a different angle. It is impossible to tell if Gray has possession of the ball.

Gray is on the ground. Fischer is over him. The ball is in the air.

Only afterward was Referee Silva's dilemma placed in proper focus. In his conference with the other officials, two of them stated that Gray caught the ball in the end zone and fumbled the ball after he hit the ground. Their signal for a touchdown would have been correct if that's what actually happened. Once in the end zone, a player need retain possession only a fraction as long as he would between the two goal lines. A third official signaled "no touchdown" because, even though he did not see the play in its entirety, he observed Gray hitting the ground without the ball. To him, Gray lost possession of the ball on the way to hitting the turf.

The "possession" interpretation is the key to the ruling. Silva obviously accepted the majority rule, which photographs and instant replay proved to be incorrect. Gray did have possession of the ball in the air, but he did not have the ball as he hit the ground. St. Louis won the game and went on to win their conference title, but Redskins' fans still believe they lost Super Bowl possibilities because of an incorrect call.

51

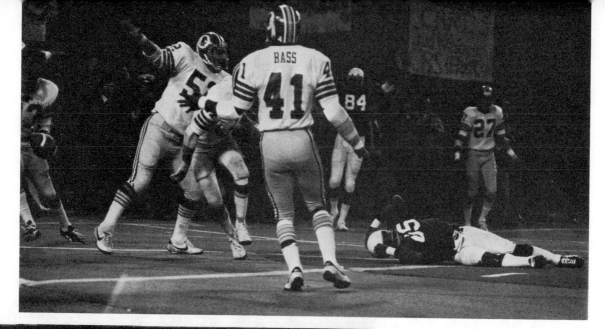

The ball has bounced away (extreme left) and the Redskins are already protesting that Gray did not have full possession. Gray grabs his helmet, unsure whether the catch is legal.

The officials confer and the Cardinal and Redskin players await the decision. It was finally ruled that Gray had possession and it was called a touchdown. The Cardinals went on to win the game in overtime and the Redskins did not make the playoff.

The Miami Dolphins–Buffalo Bills game on December 1, 1975, was billed as the contest that would decide the Eastern Division title. Miami was in first place with an 8–3 record, and Buffalo and the Baltimore Colts were tied for second with identical 7–4 records.

Trailing 21–0 at halftime, Buffalo charged back in the second half and narrowed Miami's lead to 3 points, 24–21, in the fourth quarter. Miami had the ball on their own 28-yard line, trying to hang on to possession. On the second down, Mercury Morris of the Dolphins swept around right end and

52

fumbled. Pat Toomay of the Bills rushed to recover the ball, and in his mad dash he bumped headlinesman Jerry Bergman in the scramble. Toomay had apparently not heard that the play had been blown dead before the fumble. Bergman, apparently thinking that Toomay had hit him intentionally, called for a 15-yard "unsportsmanlike conduct" penalty.

Instead of a third down and 7 yards to go deep in their own territory, Miami now had a first down and was in good field position. Two plays later, Miami's Don Nottingham burst 56 yards for a touchdown, to ensure the Dolphin victory.

The confusing part of the decision was that if Toomay was in fact guilty of "unsportsmanlike conduct," it called for his removal from the game. Toomay was not ejected, headlinesman Bergman explained, because "discretion" kept him from removing one of Buffalo's star players.

The damage was done. Perhaps if "instant replay" had been at Bergman's disposal, he would not have invoked the penalty. It is logical to assume that if Bergman had seen the play again, he could have understood more readily that he obstructed Toomay's path to the fumbled ball and that Toomay, as practically every football player has done in the past, pushed aside any obstacle in his way.

Ironically, the Buffalo loss did as much good for Baltimore as it did for Miami. Of the three, only Buffalo did not find its way into the 1975 playoffs.

Perhaps the greatest controversy of the 1975 season took place in the first round of the postseason playoffs: the game between the Dallas Cowboys and the Minnesota Vikings.

Minnesota, predicted to meet the Pittsburgh Steelers in the Super Bowl, was hanging on to a 14–10 lead over Dallas with the clock showing only thirty-two seconds left. Getting the ball into field-goal position would do the Cowboys no good, so Minnesota, the spectators, and the millions watching the game on television knew that the Cowboys would have to throw a long desperation pass in the vicinity of the end zone and then pray that the 1000-to-1 chance would pay off.

Since the Minnesota defense was prepared to give away short-pass receptions as long as their goal line wasn't threatened, Dallas quarterback Roger Staubach's chances of pulling off the perfect play for a game-winning touchdown were slim. Never did Staubach think, when he faded back for his all-or-nothing toss, that an "imperfect play" would give them a victory.

53

Staubach's pass arched toward the goal line. Drew Pearson awaited the battle he would have with Minnesota safety Nate Wright. Wright had the advantage of not having to run stride for stride with Pearson and perhaps being outrun if the pass was perfect. Rather, Wright could observe the play as it progressed before him and await Pearson and the ball in the luxury of knowing that he would be responsible for batting down the ball that would send the Vikings into the next round toward Super Bowl glory.

The fact that Staubach's throw was shorter than intended took away Wright's advantage. Pearson, still able to observe the flight of the ball as he dashed down the sideline, was able to backtrack and go up for the ball. Wright, surprised that Pearson was not going to meet him at the intended spot, recovered and joined Pearson in the battle for the ball.

Pearson was able to lunge over Wright's right shoulder, and incredibly, the ball wedged between his hip and elbow. Meanwhile, his timing off because of the underthrow, Nate Wright went sprawling to the ground as Pearson went scampering into the end zone.

Pearson looked around like the proverbial boy caught with his hand in the cookie jar. Surely, he must have thought, there was no way for him to be standing in the end zone legally. Automatically, he looked for the ominous sign from the official that he had committed an offensive infraction that gave him sole possession of the ball in the end zone.

There was no sign from the officials. Pearson's catch was legal, and the stunned Vikings stood around helplessly, knowing the game was lost.

This is the controversial NFC playoff game in which the Dallas Cowboys knock the Minnesota Vikings out of the playoffs. Roger Staubach of the Cowboys (with arm extended) has just thrown a long desperation pass toward the end zone.

The pass is short; Cowboy receiver Drew Pearson retreats and becomes entangled with Viking defender Nate Wright.

Pearson, on the 5-yard line, has the ball as Wright goes down. Paul Krause of the Vikings comes over to assist Wright.

Pearson jogs to the goal line.

56

Pearson scores and looks around to see if he will be called for offensive interference.

The Cowboys mob Drew Pearson. Preston Pearson (No. 26 and no relation) joins in the celebration.

4.
Jack Sharkey Deserved Better

JACK SHARKEY WAS PROBABLY THE MOST CON-troversial heavyweight boxer in the history of the sport. So many of his major bouts ended under clouds of suspicion that he never truly earned his proper place as one of the best heavyweights of all time. In six years, 1927 through 1933, he was involved in five bouts with famous heavyweights of the day. All of them ended in major furors.

Sharkey was born Joseph Paul Zukauskas of Lithuanian parents in 1902. He served in the U.S. Navy after World War I and took up boxing aboard ship. On his discharge he began fighting in the Boston area and took the name of Jack Sharkey. Rumor has it that the name was a combination of two of his idols: "Jack" was from Jack Dempsey and "Sharkey" from Tom Sharkey, another former Boston sailor who fought around the turn of the century.

Sharkey was smart, fast, and he could hit. But he had a terrible temper and usually engaged in some type of tantrum after every fight, whether he won or lost. Sharkey first gained national fame by being knocked out.

On September 23, 1926, Jack Dempsey lost his heavyweight title on a ten-round decision to Gene Tunney. Famed promoter Tex Rickard knew he would have to build Dempsey up again for the public to accept a return Tunney-Dempsey bout. Jack Sharkey was the man chosen for Dempsey to gain back his credibility.

Sharkey's prominence now grew when he beat Harry Wills, the man Dempsey continually avoided while he was champion. Wills was known as "The Black Menace," and boxing was not ready for another black champion so soon after Jack Johnson's five-year reign had prompted the "White Hope" mentality.

Dempsey was so soundly beaten by Tunney in their first fight that very few gave him a chance against Sharkey. The thirty-two-year-old Dempsey was an underdog in the betting; and of twenty-five sportswriters polled before the fight, sixteen selected Sharkey.

The Sharkey-Dempsey fight took place at New York's Yankee Stadium on July 21, 1927 with 75,000 people paying more than a million dollars. In the early rounds Sharkey was doing the same job on Dempsey that Tunney had done nine months before. Dempsey's nose was bloodied, and he could see out of only one eye.

For almost six rounds the Sharkey pounding had made Dempsey rubber-legged. With the sixth round coming to a close, the proposed Tunney-Dempsey return bout was in jeopardy. As the bell sounded ending round six, Dempsey smashed Sharkey twice. Sharkey, angered, came back with a hard right to Dempsey's face. Most of the crowd saw only Sharkey's late punch. All 75,000 fans booed the Boston fighter loudly.

In the seventh round Sharkey continued jabbing Dempsey all over the ring. During a clinch, Dempsey pounded Sharkey's midsection at the beltline. Sharkey stepped back, turned his head, and protested to the referee, Jack O'Sullivan, that Dempsey was hitting below the belt. With Sharkey's head turned, Dempsey landed a tremendous left hook to Sharkey's jaw. Sharkey went down for the full count.

After the fight, boxing experts at ringside were almost equally divided in their opinion of Dempsey's blows. The *New York Times* polled the experts and printed a scorecard of their opinions.

When New York State Boxing Commissioner James J. Farley announced that he had seen no foul and that Dempsey would remain the winner, the Dempsey-Tunney return bout was assured. Two months later, the famed Tunney-Dempsey "long count" affair took place with Tunney retaining the championship.

Dempsey wanted no more of Tunney, so Tex Rickard needed a new challenger for the champion. A New Zealand heavyweight named Tom Heeney had made a name for himself with knockouts over Jim Maloney and Johnny Risko. He, along with Sharkey, were the only names Rickard believed the public would accept as a challenger for Tunney.

Sharkey and Heeney had fought to a draw, but it was well known that Rickard believed that a Tunney-Sharkey bout would bring in a bigger payday than a match between Tunney and the New Zealander. However, one of the worst kept secrets of the day was that Tunney wanted no part of Sharkey, because Sharkey was *too* good, just as Dempsey had continually refused to meet Harry Wills during the time he was champion. So a Tunney-Heeney bout was set for July 26, 1928.

Both Rickard and Tunney were correct. The bout was a financial loss, and Tunney gave a terrible beating to Heeney. Tunney then put the heavyweight scene into its worst dilemma in years by retiring as undefeated champion of the world.

With the crown now vacant, the National Boxing Association (NBA) and the New York State Boxing Commission ordered that a series of elimination bouts be held among the top contenders. Sharkey, a young German heavyweight named Max Schmeling, and the British titleholder, Phil Scott, emerged as the three final contenders.

On February 27, 1930, Sharkey met Scott in Miami. For the second time in less than three years, Sharkey was to be involved in a major controversy.

Scott won the first round, but Jack put the British champion down in the second. In the third round Sharkey went to the attack again. He suddenly leaped forward and hit Scott with a left to the jaw and a right to the midsection. Scott went down holding his right side and protesting to Referee Lou Magnolia that Sharkey had hit him a low blow. Scott went down twice more in the round. Each time, he protested to Magnolia that he was fouled. After the third knockdown of the round, Scott was writhing on the canvas. Magnolia motioned for Scott to get up and fight. Scott refused. Magnolia finally gave Scott one more crack at getting up, but the Britisher refused. Magnolia then awarded Sharkey the bout on a technical knockout in the third round.

Years later, the "instant replay" of the final Sharkey blow seems to indicate that Scott was hit fairly and that the British champion was living up to his nickname of "Feinting Phil." It seems that Scott more than once in his career had been the victim of blows that were invisible to spectators and officials alike.

Jack Dempsey pummels Jack Sharkey at the beltline
in the seventh round of their fight in 1927.

Sharkey protests to referee Jack
O'Sullivan that Dempsey hit him
below the belt. O'Sullivan moves
in to try to separate the two fighters.

Dempsey hits Sharkey with a
tremendous left to the head
that knocks Sharkey out.

Photo sequence shows Jack Sharkey (left) leaping forward and catching Phil Scott with a left to the jaw and a right to the midsection in the third round of their 1930 bout. Scott goes to the canvas claiming the right hand was below the belt. Referee Lou Magnolia told Scott the blows were legal. Scott went down twice more during the round, continually claiming that Sharkey hit him low. Referee Magnolia disallowed Scott's protests. When Magnolia ordered Scott to get up and continue the fight, Scott refused. Magnolia then awarded the bout to Sharkey on a technical knockout.

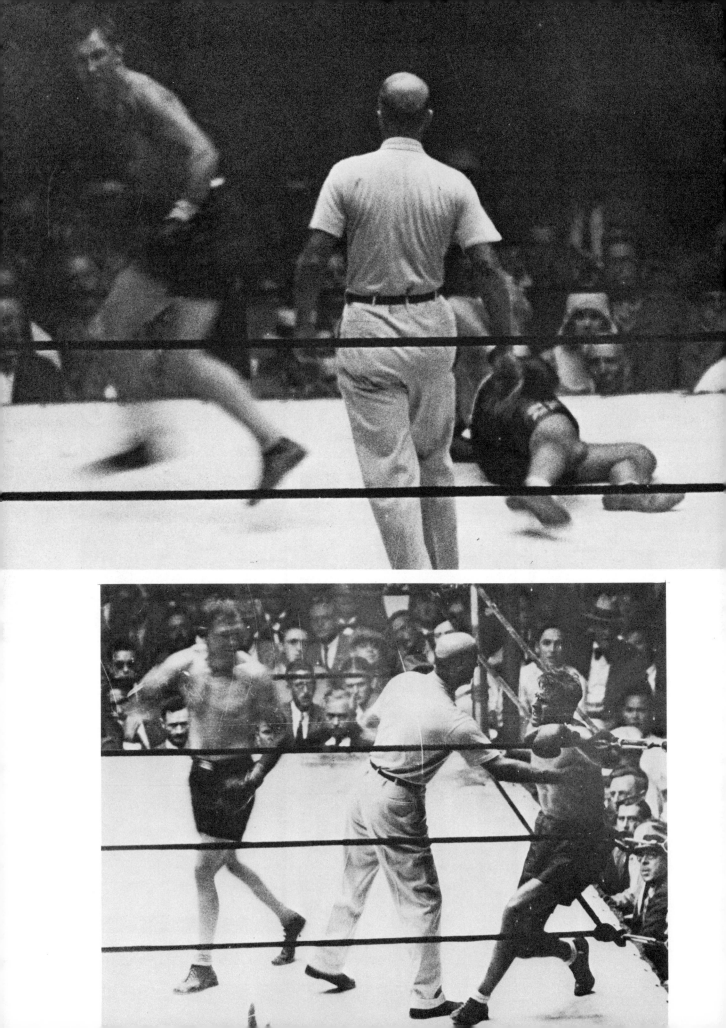

Three months and ten days later, Sharkey met Max Schmeling for the heavyweight championship of the world. Sharkey was ahead after three rounds and looked well on his way to the title. But at the end of the fourth round Sharkey threw a vicious left to the beltline, and Schmeling went down in obvious pain. It looked almost like a duplication of the Sharkey-Scott fiasco of a few months before. However, this time the referee, Jim Crowley, was in no position to see where the punch landed.

With Schmeling on the canvas, his manager, Joe Jacobs, came rushing into the ring screaming that Schmeling had been fouled and that Sharkey should be disqualified.

Referee Crowley was getting attacked from all sides. Joe Jacobs was screaming "Foul" and calling for Sharkey's disqualification. Crowley then began questioning the two judges, Harold Barnes and Charles Mathison.

Even today there is no clear account as to how Crowley made his final decision. All the crowd knew was that Crowley had counted to "five" over the fallen Schmeling when the bell rang ending the round. Finally the ring announcer, Joe Humphreys, proclaimed that Sharkey had been disqualified for the low blow and that Schmeling was the new heavyweight champion of the world.

James Dawson, the respected boxing reporter for the *New York Times,* apparently gives much of the credit to Judge Harold Barnes in the decision that gave Schmeling the title. The following day Dawson's by-line story reported:

> Outstanding in this momentous situation was Judge Barnes, a medium-sized man, slim quiet man who faced perhaps the most trying situation a modern ring has produced, and gave the decision as he saw it. . . . Judge Barnes had the courage of his convictions.

Then Dawson gave his own opinion:

> . . . I was advantageously seated to the left of Judge Barnes and the action was directly above me and I can say that the left hook Sharkey directed for the body landed foul and merited disqualification because of its obvious disabling effect.

John Durant, in his book *The Heavyweight Champions,* wrote:

> Although Max wore a protector which had been proved to withstand the hardest blow without harm to the wearer, he

Sequence on this and the following page shows Jack Sharkey winding up and throwing a tremendous left to the midsection that has Max Schmeling screaming with pain in their 1930 championship bout. Sharkey was disqualified and Max Schmeling was named champion of the world.

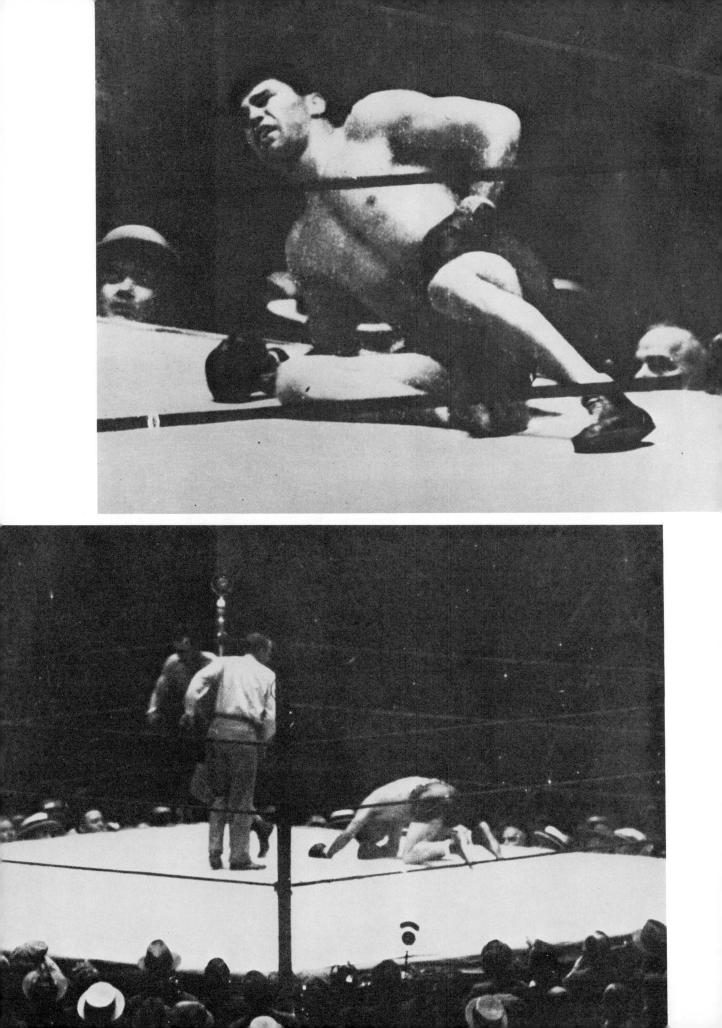

went into a grimacing act on the canvas that would have drawn applause from the Barrymores. . . . Crowley was stunned and confused. He looked for help from the two ringside judges, Harold Barnes and Charles Mathison. Crowley conferred with both men. Neither were sure about the foul.

Durant then went on to write:

Was Schmeling really fouled? A careful study of the movies by unbiased observers later revealed that the blow was not low. It was on the beltline; close to foul territory perhaps, but certainly not in the groin.

However, the *New York Times* of Saturday, June 14, 1930, headlined: SHARKEY'S PUNCH PLAINLY REVEALED AS FOUL BY MOVIES OF TITLE BOUT WITH SCHMELING.

Mat Fleischer, perhaps boxing's most respected historian, wrote in *A Pictorial History of Boxing:* "Neither Harold Barnes, a judge, nor the referee had seen the low punch, but Charles.F. Mathison, the other judge, agreed with Schmeling."

Every account seemed to differ. Much credit for Referee Crowley's final decision is given to Arthur Brisbane, the famed editor of the Hearst newspaper chain. From his ringside seat, Brisbane shouted up to Crowley that he would personally see that boxing would be outlawed unless Sharkey was disqualified.

A direct result of the Sharkey-Schmeling fiasco was the introduction of the "no foul" rule by New York Boxing Commissioner James J. Farley. The new rule stated that a man knocked to the canvas would be counted out whether the blow was fair or foul. This put an end to the "invisible" punches that highlighted many of the fights of the era.

The logical rematch between Schmeling and Sharkey took more than two years to come about. On June 21, 1932, the two met again. This time, Schmeling was on the receiving end of what to most observers was the worst decision in years.

They fought fifteen rounds in what was considered a dull fight. To most, Schmeling clearly had the advantage. Nevertheless, the two judges split their vote, and the fight was awarded to Sharkey when the referee, Gunboat Smith, gave a ruling in his favor. Sharkey had at last become heavyweight champion in what was one of the worst performances of his career. It was after this fight that Schmeling's manager, Joe Jacobs, came out with his famous "We wuz robbed."

In between his two fights with Schmeling, Sharkey tuned up with a fifteen-rounder with Primo Carnera. Sharkey won easily. Carnera was a 6-foot 5¾-inch, 250-pound giant with no ability. He was a freak of the ring, but he had been carefully promoted as an awesome terror. The truth of the matter was that Carnera could hardly fight, but he built up a record against stumblebums that vaulted him into prominence.

It was constantly rumored that Carnera's career was carefully controlled by the underworld and that many of his fights were won before he ever entered the ring; his opponents were either paid off or threatened with violence to the point that a Carnera victory was a foregone conclusion.

Carnera became Sharkey's first title defense. The champion had stayed out of action a full year after beating Schmeling. Sharkey and Carnera met on June 29, 1933, and the fight still is the most controversial on Sharkey's record.

For five dull rounds Sharkey outpointed Carnera and seemed well on his way to a duplication of his first victory. The sixth round went as the previous five. Suddenly, Sharkey was down and out. The ending was bizarre. Hardly anybody saw the knockout punch.

The "instant replay" of the knockout punch clearly shows Carnera throwing a short right uppercut, then hitting Sharkey with a left as the champion was on his way down. But the practically unanimous decision from all who were there was that Sharkey was a victim of another one of Carnera's famous "invisible" punches.

The rumored Carnera underworld associations and the known fact that he was a third-rate fighter, combined with the fact that Sharkey was one of the best heavyweights of his time, prompted famed sports editor Dan Parker to write: "Every time Jack Sharkey hears or reads of Primo's name, he should hang his head in shame."

It was a sad epitaph to the career of a man whom many believed to have been better than Jack Dempsey or Gene Tunney.

Jack Sharkey, again champion, meets Primo Carnera for the second time. Earlier, Sharkey had won an easy decision. For five rounds, Sharkey outpointed Carnera and seemed well on his way to a repeat victory. In the sixth round, Carnera hit Sharkey with a short right uppercut that sent Sharkey reeling. As Sharkey was on his way down to the canvas, Carnera scored with a left and the champion was out. Very few experts at ringside thought Carnera's punches were capable of that much damage.

75

Carnera standing over fallen Jack Sharkey.

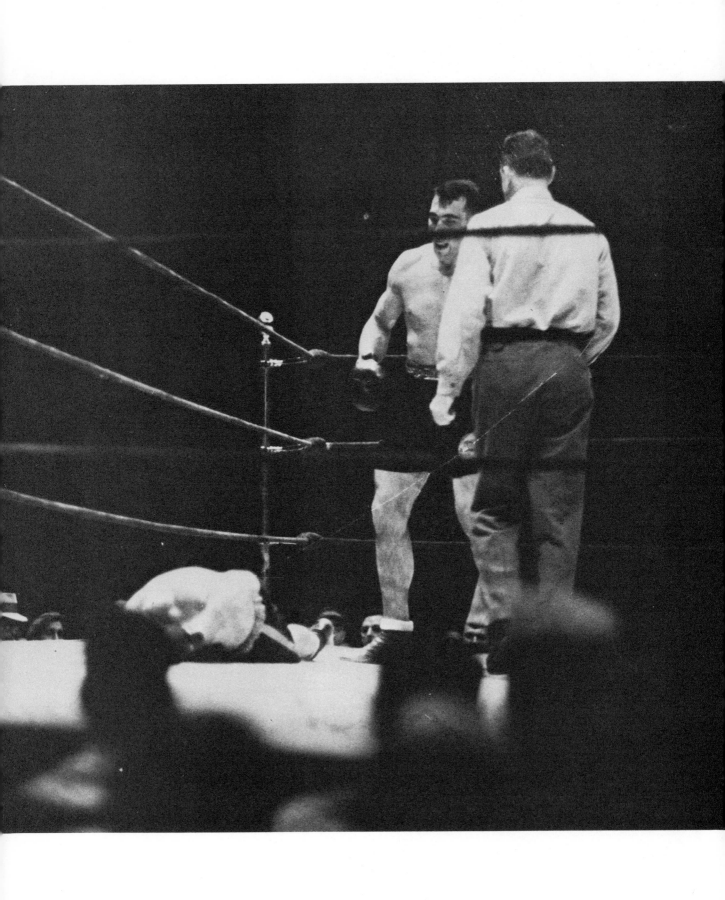

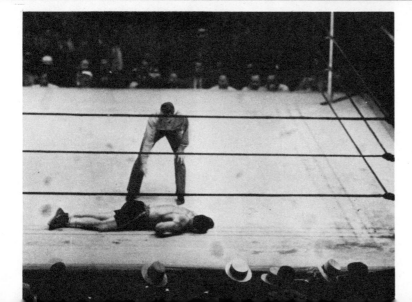

5.
Olympic Big Ones That Got Away

A FEW MINUTES BEFORE THE 100-METER FINAL AT the Berlin Olympic Games of 1936, a reporter asked the great American sprinter Jesse Owens what his thoughts were. As he took off his sweat suit, Jesse replied sadly, "A lifetime of training for just ten seconds."

Owens was a fortunate Olympian. He went on to win four gold medals and to become the outstanding performer of the Berlin Olympic Games. But for many Olympic finalists, the lifetime of training ends unhappily by an infinitesimal part of a second. Unfortunately for them, photo-finish cameras and electrical timers combine to deprive them of Olympic immortality.

The most frustrated Olympic competitor of all time was Herb McKenley of Jamaica. At the London Olympic Games of 1948, McKenley was entered in three final events. In the first event, the 200-meter run, he finished fourth, only two-tenths of a second behind the gold-medal winner, Mel Patton of the United States.

A few days later, he was the heavy favorite to win the 400-meter race. As world record holder in that event, he was considered the most certain gold-medal winner of the Games. McKenley led for 395 meters. In the last five meters, his teammate Arthur Wint caught him and went on to win by a foot.

Three days later, McKenley was scheduled to run the final leg of the 1600-meter relay. His team, Jamaica, and the United States were co-favorites. As he waited for the final passoff, tragedy struck. Arthur Wint, running the third leg, pulled up lame. McKenley never had a chance to run.

Four years later, at the Helsinki Olympics, McKenley was again entered in three events. In the 100 meters, McKenley and Lindy Remigino of the United States crossed the finish line as one. Remigino was certain McKenley had nipped him at the tape and came over to congratulate him. However, the officials called for the photo-finish photograph. After several hours' delay, Remigino was named the winner. McKenley was given the same finishing time as the gold-medal winner, but again he had to settle for second place.

Herb McKenley (No. 90) finishes two-tenths of a second behind the winner, Mel Patton (No. 71), in the 200-meter final at the London Olympics.

Arthur Wint (No. 122) of Jamaica defeats his teammate,
Herb McKenley (No. 90), by a foot in the 400-meter final
at the 1948 London Olympic Games.

Lindy Remigino of the United
States (third from the top)
defeats Herb McKenley of
Jamaica (second from the top),
in the 100-meter final at the 1952
Helsinki Olympics.

George Rhoden of Jamaica defeats teammate McKenley
in the 400-meter final at the Helsinki games.

Two days later, McKenley was a finalist in his favorite event, the 400 meters. His teammate George Rhoden crossed the finish line in front of him by a few inches. Herb McKenley again missed winning a gold medal by a margin that could be detected only by a photo-finish picture.

A few days later, McKenley had his sixth attempt for a gold medal, as a member of the 1600-meter relay team. The Jamaican team was the same quartet of runners that ran into tragic circumstances four years before. This time, McKenley ran the third leg and was able to make up a fifteen-yard deficit to give Jamaica a one-foot lead. Then George Rhoden, who had defeated him a few days before in the 400-meter race, was able to hold off the challenge of Mal Whitfield of the United States, to give Jamaica the victory. After six tries, Herb McKenley had at last won a gold medal—and this time he didn't even have to cross the finish line.

Jack Davis of Southern California was the unluckiest hurdler in Olympic history. At the 1952 Helsinki Games, in the 110-meter hurdles, he matched Harrison Dillard of the United States stride for stride until the last hurdle. Davis nicked the last barrier, which slowed him up just enough to give Dillard a photo-finish victory. So close was the finish that both men were timed in an Olympic record of 13.7.

Four years later, at the Melbourne Olympics, Jack Davis ran a perfect race. He skimmed over every hurdle in perfect form and was timed in a new Olympic record of 13.5. However, Lee Calhoun of the United States also ran a perfect race, and he too was timed in an Olympic record of 13.5. Again, Jack Davis had to wait for the judging of the photo-finish picture.

As Davis and Calhoun walked nervously to the infield, Davis seemed to sense the outcome. He congratulated Calhoun. Shortly after, the judges came out with the decision that Calhoun had won by an inch. In two successive Olympic Games, Jack Davis had lost a gold medal in photo finishes, but on each occasion, he was given the same finishing time as the gold-medal winner.

Davis finally did win a photo finish, but it wasn't Jack Davis. At the Rome Olympics of 1960, Otis Davis of the United States and Carl Kaufmann of Germany hit the finish line together in the final of the 400 meters. Davis, who had led most of the way, was certain that he was beaten at the finish. He sat on a bench waiting for the bad news. When it finally was announced that he had held on just long enough to win, he

Jack Davis of the United States (on the extreme right)
is defeated by Harrison Dillard of the United States, in
the 110-meter hurdles at Helsinki. Both were given the
same time.

couldn't believe it. Davis kept questioning his teammates to make certain. Finally, the electric scoreboard confirmed it. Davis and Kaufmann had finished in the same exact time, but Davis was an inch ahead at the tape.

But of all the photo finishes in Olympic history, nothing could compare to the 400-meter individual medley final in swimming at the Munich Olympic Games of 1972, when Gunnar Larsson of Sweden and Tim McKee of the United States touched the wall at the finish in what appeared to the naked eye was a perfect dead heat.

As in all recent Olympiads, the race was decided instantaneously by an electric timing device. Immediately the results were flashed on the scoreboard: both men had touched the wall in the time of 4:31.98. The judges decided to carry the sophisticated timing apparatus one step further. As Larsson and McKee waited at the pool's edge, a new set of numbers was flashed on the scoreboard. Gunnar Larsson had touched 2/1000 *of a second* before McKee.

Lee Calhoun of the United States (right) defeats Jack Davis at the finish line in the 110-meter hurdles in Melbourne. Again, Davis was given the same time as the winner. In two Olympic 110-meter hurdle finals, Davis finished in the same time as the winner but twice had to settle for the silver medal.

89

Otis Davis, United States, defeats Carl Kaufmann of Germany in the 400-meter final in Rome. It took the judges ten minutes to separate the two at the finish. Both were given the same time.

```
1.LARSSON,GUNNAR   SWE    4:31.981
2.MCKEE,TIM        USA    4:31.983
3.HARGITAY,ANDRA   HUN    4:32.70
4.FURNISS,STEVEN   USA    4:35.44
5.HALL,GARY        USA    4:37.38
6.GINGSJOE,BENGT   SWE    4:37.96
7.WINDEATT,GRAHA   AUS    4:40.39
8.SPERLING,WOLFR   GDR    4:40.66
```

Results from the 400-meter individual medley are posted on the scoreboard. Gunnar Larsson first, Tim McKee second.

Ironically, it was the *lack* of sophisticated timing machinery that, in 1960, lost a gold medal for Lance Larsen of the United States. In this controversial finish, all six timers caught Larsen finishing at least one-tenth of a second faster than John Devitt of Australia. However, because electrical timing had not yet been introduced into the Olympic Games for swimming, the finishes were decided by judges sitting at the side of the pool. They did not see Larsen's underwater touch at the finish.

Devitt was given the nod by the majority of judges. This was the first time in Olympic history that a gold medal was awarded to an athlete who swam slower than the second-place finisher.

92

6.
A Few Moments from Olympic Gold

THE 1932 LOS ANGELES OLYMPICS WERE THE MOST controversial in the eight decades of competition that followed the modern revival of the Games in Athens in 1896. To this day, many believe that no fewer than three gold medals were awarded to the wrong athletes. By use of modern "instant replay" techniques, it is possible to clear up much of the mystery surrounding the results that have clouded the final decisions rendered at the 1932 Games.

The first controversy took place on August 1, the final of the men's 100-meter dash.

Ralph Metcalfe and Eddie Tolan of the United States had won all their preliminary and semifinal heats and were the prerace choices. Metcalfe was given a slight edge because he had defeated Tolan twice in the Olympic trials in both the 100-meter and 200-meter dashes.

Metcalfe, a notoriously poor starter, trailed Tolan throughout the first 90 meters. But as they roared to the tape in the final 10 meters, it was evident that Metcalfe was faster. It was now only a matter of whether Tolan could hold him off.

Tolan and Metcalfe broke the tape together. From the stands, it appeared that Metcalfe was inches ahead. This illusion obviously was caused by the fact that Metcalfe was clearly in front one foot past the finish line.

The finish-line officials went into a huddle, but there was little discussion in the press box. The near-unanimous opinion was that Metcalfe had gotten there first. So certain were the wire services that they sent the news around the world that Ralph Metcalfe had won the gold medal.

As the minutes went by without an official announcement, it became evident that the judges were not as certain as those in the press box. Finally, the officials called for the photo-finish camera to make the decision for them. It was being used for the first time in Olympic competition.

The device was the Kirby Two-Eyed Camera, and it was a technological marvel of its day. It was the brainchild of Gustavus T. Kirby, president emeritus of the United States Olympic Committee, who collaborated with electrical engineers of Western Electric to produce a motion-picture camera that could be operated at 128 frames per second. The camera was placed on a tower at the finish line, twenty-five feet above the ground. The Kirby Two-Eyed Camera was capable of printing the positions of the runners a few inches *before* the finish line, at the finish line, and a few inches *after* the finish line.

To the officials observing the photograph that froze the runners at the finish line, there was no question that the race was a dead heat. The chests of both Metcalfe and Tolan hit the tape at *exactly* the same moment. The officials were in a dilemma. Never in the history of the Olympic Games had there been a dead heat in track and field competition.

This fact, in addition to the rules that prevailed in 1932, provided the officials with good reason to go one step further. For the 1932 rules under which the Olympic Games were contested stated that the winner of a race "shall be the contestant whose *torso* is first across the finish line." (Italics mine—author.) It was decided to print the frame of film taken *after* Metcalfe and Tolan had broken the tape with their chests. Eddie Tolan was named the winner.

In the photographs used to decide the finish, an incredible phenomenon takes place. The first frame shows Metcalfe and Tolan hitting the tape at the same time. *Both torsos* have still not passed over the finish line.

To the judges, the second photograph showed that Tolan's *entire torso* had crossed the finish line but that Metcalfe's torso is still behind the line. Years later, Ralph Metcalfe would comment wryly that he lost the race because "I had a bigger fanny."

The race is still considered controversial because the explanation of the judges' decision was not prominently reported

the following day. Gustavus Kirby gave the following explanation: "The rules *do not* accept the tape as the finish line. The finish is *the line* painted across the track."

Kirby's explanation went on to state that the judges placed a ruler across the finish line, making certain it also covered the white post that supports the tape. (The reader can duplicate this method.) The white post and finish line were to be at precise right angles. When this is done, it can be seen that there is daylight between Tolan's torso and the white post, which means that his body had passed over the finish line. However, the same ruler dissects Metcalfe's back. To the judges, this meant that Metcalfe's torso had still not passed the finish line. The only possible explanation is that Tolan leaned forward as he hit the finish tape. It must also be mentioned that the line dissects both Tolan and Metcalfe at the buttocks.

Eddie Tolan (top) and Ralph Metcalfe appear to be neck and neck one meter from the finish line during the 100-meter run at the Lost Angeles Olympic Games.

95

Official photograph of the final of the 100 meters. Eddie Tolan (top) and Ralph Metcalfe hit the tape simultaneously.

One main fact justifies Metcalfe's sharing the gold medal with Tolan. If the white post that supports the finish-line tape was the deciding factor in regard to Tolan's torso being over the finish line, it was incumbent upon the officials to make certain that the white post was accurately checked after the race to be precisely at a right angle with the finish line. The post was not checked. Yet the slightest deviation, by even a fraction of an inch, could have changed Tolan's position radically since he was closer to the post.

These many years later, Metcalfe has additional good reason to be upset over the 1932 decision. Just one hour before the final was held, the two semifinal heats were run. Metcalfe and Tolan were declared the winners in their individual heats. There was no question of Metcalfe's victory. But a previously unpublished photograph of Tolan's semifinal "victory" has recently been discovered. The photograph clearly shows that Tolan finished *third* behind Daniel Joubert of South Africa and Takoyoshi Yoshioka of Japan. In fact, Tolan was only *two feet* away from being eliminated from the final by the fourth-place runner, H. Wright.

Eddie Tolan died in 1971 and never commented on the controversial finish. Ralph Metcalfe, now a congressman from Illinois, still regrets not sharing the gold medal.

The photograph that decided the 100-meter final was taken one frame later. Eddie Tolan has managed to get his entire torso across the finish line while Metcalfe's back still has not crossed over. According to 1932 rules, first place is awarded to the runner whose entire torso is over the line even though both break the tape at the same time.

Another angle of the finish. Tolan at the bottom and Metcalfe in the middle.

An earlier decision by the officials in a semi-final of the 100 meters, run a few hours before the controversial final. Daniel Joubert of South Africa (closest to the camera) and Takoyoshi Yoshioka of Japan finish in a virtual dead heat. But Eddie Tolan (alongside Joubert) is called the winner; Joubert places second, and Yoshioka third. In reality, Tolan was just two feet away from being eliminated from the final, since only three men from each semi-final qualify for the final, and the fourth-place finisher, H. Wright (alongside Yoshioka), passed Tolan a few feet beyond the finish line.

Eddie Tolan wins the 200 meters in Los Angeles. Ralph Metcalfe is in third place, behind George Simpson of the United States. Metcalfe claimed that his lane had been measured incorrectly by nine feet, the approximate distance Tolan had on him at the finish.

"Eddie Tolan was one of my closest friends," says Metcalfe, "and he had nothing to do with it. But I heard afterward that the officials believed that I was a certain winner in the 200 meters and that it would be nice to give the gold medal to Eddie Tolan since this was going to be his last Olympics."

With one gold medal lost, Metcalfe ran into additional horror two days later in the final of the 200 meters. Eddie Tolan won his second gold medal, followed by George Simpson of the United States. Metcalfe was third. After the race, however, rumors began circulating throughout the Olympic village that Metcalfe's lane had been measured incorrectly, that in fact he had to run eight to ten feet farther than anybody else in the race.

"I didn't know this was a handicap race," Metcalfe says now. "There is no question that I had to run a longer distance than anybody else in the race."

The official photograph of the finish shows Tolan approximately three yards ahead of Metcalfe. Transposed, this becomes nine feet—*the extra distance Metcalfe purportedly had to run* because of the incorrectly measured lane.

In two races Metcalfe had won a silver and a bronze medal, but circumstances had prevented him from winning the gold. Four years later, Metcalfe finally won his gold. After finishing second to Jesse Owens in the 100 meters, he joined Owens and two other teammates as part of the 400-meter relay team that defeated Germany and Italy in world record time.

The 5,000-meter race at the 1932 Olympics caused an even greater controversy than the earlier races. It took place on August 5, four days after the 100-meter final and just two days after Metcalfe's claim that his 200-meter lane was measured incorrectly.

Lauri Lehtinen of Finland, the world record holder, was the favorite in the race. Lehtinen was the latest of the Flying Finns to dominate the 5,000 meters since it was first run at the Stockholm Games of 1912. Then Hannes Kolehmainen won the middle triumph of his three gold medals. The others were the 10,000 meters and the 10,000-meter cross country. Paavo Nurmi, Finland's greatest Olympic champion, won the 5,000 meters in 1924; his perennial shadow, Villie Ritola, came home first in 1928.

Finnish runners had won three of the four 5,000-meter races run to date, and Lauri Lehtinen, who just a few months before had shattered Paavo Nurmi's world record, was a heavy favorite to continue the Finnish dominance.

In a preliminary heat, two days before the final, Ralph Hill of Klamath Falls, Oregon, created a mild surprise by breaking Nurmi's 1924 Olympic record by a little more than one second. In second place was Lauri Lehtinen, about ten meters behind.

The Hill victory over Lehtinen was not considered a threat to the Finnish world record holder. Lehtinen, never giving Hill a serious challenge, was content to qualify and save his energy for the final.

Fourteen men qualified for the final. The 5,000-meter distance would require traveling the 400-meter Los Angeles Coliseum track twelve and a half times.

For two-thirds of the race, Lehtinen and his teammate, Lauri Virtanen, took turns setting the pace. With three and a half laps to go, Hill moved between the two Finns into second place. The three ran in Indian file within a meter of each other. On the next to last lap, Lauri Virtanen was struggling and dropped back some thirty yards behind Lehtinen and Hill. Now it became a two-man race. With three hundred meters to go, Lehtinen began his final drive. Hill stayed right with him. Coming off the final turn, Lehtinen was on the inside, still a meter in front of Hill, who was in lane 2, just off Lehtinen's right shoulder.

Hill was preparing for one final surge that would perhaps carry him past the tiring Lehtinen. At the precise moment that Hill was making his move, Lehtinen came off the turn to move into Hill's lane, blocking the American's path. Hill was forced to hold up, breaking his stride. But he quickly moved inside, into the lane vacated by Lehtinen. Lehtinen, still in full stride, was able to increase the distance between them.

Hill started another surge, trying to make up the ground he had lost when Lehtinen changed lanes. As they came down the stretch, with Lehtinen about three meters in front, the crowd started to roar its disapproval. In the middle of the stretch, the near-exhausted Lehtinen slowly began to move back to his original inside lane. The roars from the 80,000 spectators grew louder as they approached the tape. With about ten meters to go, Hill made one final sprint. At the tape, Lehtinen was still one foot in front.

The Los Angeles Coliseum was in an uproar. A crescendo of jeers resounded throughout the stadium. The spectators were calling for the disqualification of Lehtinen.

The roars became louder. For several minutes there was fear that a riot might ensue unless the officials took some positive action against Lehtinen. Finally, Bill Henry, the technical director of the Games, spoke calmly over the public address system: "Ladies and Gentlemen, please remember that these people are our guests."

Immediately the derisive sounds from the crowd stopped. A smattering of applause was the token response to the announcement.

Two hours went by before the decision was announced. Lauri Lehtinen was declared the winner with Ralph Hill in second place. Both men were given the exact same time.

The chief judge of the track events, Arthur Holz of Germany, made the following statement: "I decide in favor of Lauri Lehtinen for first place and Ralph Hill for second place. I am of the opinion that Lauri Lehtinen did not willfully interfere with Hill at the finish."

At the victory-platform ceremony the following day, Lehtinen made a gracious offer. He beckoned Hill to stand with him on the top step of the winners' platform. Hill refused.

Nevertheless, Hill to this day handles the affair with grace and dignity. "I did not think that Lauri Lehtinen deliberately tried to keep me from the tape," he says. "He was turning around to see where I was, and I know from experience that when an exhausted man does that, he loses his sense of direction. I made no protest because I believe that Lauri Lehtinen was steering a blind course . . . wholly unintentional."

A rare film of the race was recently uncovered in the archives in Washington. It is now possible to reconstruct in frame-by-frame detail exactly what took place from the moment Lehtinen and Hill came off the final turn. And this "instant replay" conclusively shows that Lehtinen impeded Hill as they came off the turn.

Olympic rules state that the lead runner cannot cross in front of another runner unless he has a two-yard lead. At the point where Lehtinen changed lanes, he was at best one yard in front of Hill.

Once Lehtinen moved into Hill's lane, the American immediately cut to the inside lane vacated by Lehtinen. But in the changeover, Hill was forced to break his stride. Thinking Hill was still trying to pass him on the inside, Lehtinen turned his head to the right. Hill was not there. Almost in panic, Lehtinen began to move back to the inside lane. However, he noticeably slowed down either in response to the booing from the crowd or out of certainty that Hill was no longer a challenge.

With about twenty meters to go, Hill made another challenge, this time on the inside. At the finish line, he was still inches behind.

After viewing and reviewing the film in normal speed and slow motion, there are several definite conclusions:

1. It is absolutely certain that Lehtinen violated official rules by crossing in front of Hill without having a two-yard lead.

2. Hill did have to shorten his stride when he was forced to move inside.

3. Chief Judge Holz is probably correct. The films indicate that Lehtinen did not deliberately try to interfere with Hill.

It is also doubtful whether Hill could have caught Lehtinen if the race had been run properly.

The famous 5,000-meter final at the 1932 Los Angeles Olympics. Lauri Lehtinen of Finland (in black shirt) comes off the last turn a yard in front of Ralph Hill of the United States (in white shirt). Lehtinen is in the inside lane and Hill attempts to pass him on the outside.

Lehtinen is moving into Hill's lane.

As Lehtinen moves over, Hill makes a break to the inside lane vacated by Lehtinen.

Lehtinen is now in lane 2 and Hill is in the inside lane.

As they move down the stretch, Lehtinen again changes lanes and moves back to the inside.

As they move closer to the finish, Lehtinen again moves to
the outside, giving Hill an opportunity to try to move past him
on the inside.

One yard past the finish line, Lehtinen is still in front. After a long delay, the judges decide that Lehtinen's movements down the stretch did not alter the outcome of the race. Hill commented recently, "I held no bitterness then, and I hold none now."

Nevertheless, Lauri Lehtinen violated a rule by crossing in front of another runner without having the necessary two-yard lead. This violation was an important one and should have meant disqualification.

Nevertheless, the decision was made in favor of Lehtinen.

Today Ralph Hill says, "I would have liked to have stood on the winner's platform." Then, almost sadly, he adds, "But I'm not bitter about it."

Babe Didrikson, perhaps the greatest all-around woman athlete ever, was embroiled in two of the controversial finishes of the 1932 Los Angeles Games.

After winning the gold medal in the javelin, on the first day of competition, she was one of six finalists in the 80-meter hurdles. This was the first time the event would be contested at an Olympiad.

Two weeks before the Olympic Games, Babe Didrikson, at age eighteen, had amazed the world when her team, the Employers Casualty Company of Dallas, Texas, won the combined National AAU Women's Track and Field Championship and Olympic Team Trials held at Northwestern's Dyche Stadium. The term "team" championship is misleading. Babe Didrikson was the only member of the team. In less than three hours, she competed in eight of the ten events contested, winning five and tying in the sixth. Her total of 30 points gave her "team" the championship. She had earned eight more points than the total of the twenty-two-woman squad representing the Illinois Women's Athletic Club.

One of Babe's Olympic trial victories was in the 80-meter hurdles. Now in Los Angeles, she was the favorite to win the gold medal. Babe jumped the gun for a false start. As the six women regrouped, she was warned by the official starter that a second false start would eliminate her from the competition. Making certain that she wouldn't again beat the gun, Babe was last off the marks when the pistol fired.

Babe was in lane 2. Alongside her in the inside lane was her teammate, Evelyn Hall of Chicago. Hall shot out to an early lead but at the fifth hurdle, Babe caught her. They ran stride for stride over the remaining hurdles, and at the finish, Babe leaned her left shoulder forward and beat Hall by no more than an inch. The finish is controversial mainly because Evelyn Hall maintains that she beat Babe at the finish.

Again, by use of "instant replay," it is possible to confirm that Babe Didrikson was the legitimate gold-medal winner.

Through the years, Evelyn Hall continued the controversy by claiming that Babe jabbed her in the ribs as they battled over the last hurdle. The films do not show this. Moreover, Evelyn Hall claims that there was a rope burn on her neck for days after the race, the result of running through the taut finish-line tape. A photograph taken at the precise moment of the finish clearly shows both Babe Didrikson and Evelyn Hall breaking the tape with their necks.

By running the film back and forth in normal and slow-motion speed, it is possible to confirm that the officials made the right decision in naming Babe Didrikson the winner. Babe's "lean" at the finish line was the decisive factor. In the film, one frame before the finish line, the two women are exactly even. Babe was fortunate that the finish line appeared when it did.

Since film runs at 24 frames per second, Babe actually won the race by 1/24 of a second, even though both women were given the exact same time—a world record of 11.7.

But where Babe was fortunate in the 80-meter hurdles, her luck ran out in the high jump, trying for her third gold medal. She was pitted against Jean Shiley of Philadelphia. The two tied for the national title two weeks earlier at the Olympic trials.

Didrikson and Shiley matched each other height for height, eliminating the other women on the way. When they reached the height of 5 feet 5¾ inches, both Shiley and Didrikson missed all three attempts. Under the rules of the day, the officials *lowered* the bar to 5 feet 5¼ inches. The first woman to miss would have to settle for the silver medal.

Shiley jumped first and made it.

Setting her sights on the bar, Didrikson made the same familiar approach she had been making throughout the afternoon. She flew over the bar head first—the same technique she had been using throughout the competition. Immediately the officials called a conference. After a few minutes, it was announced that Babe's leap was illegal—that "diving" over the bar was not permitted under the rules.

Babe complained that she had been "diving" over the bar all afternoon. Her explanation was turned down with the frivolous comment that "none of the judges had noticed it before."

109

Babe Didrikson (second from right) leans forward with her left shoulder to break the tape and defeats her teammate Evelyn Hall (on extreme right) in the 80-meter hurdles. After the decision, Hall claimed she won, showing a rope burn on her neck as evidence that she broke the tape first.

Babe Didrikson stands on the top step of the winner's platform with her teammate Evelyn Hall, who placed second, and Marjorie Clark of South Africa, who placed third.

Because the judges hadn't "noticed" Babe's technique until the final jump, none of her other leaps was considered illegal—only the final one. She was therefore placed second behind Jean Shiley.

Today Jean Shiley maintains that she knew that Babe was jumping illegally throughout the event but that she didn't want to complain to the officials; she wanted to win the competition on the field.

Jean Shiley of Philadelphia clears the bar at 5 feet 5¾ inches to win the gold medal in the 1932 high jump. She is using the style of the day, the scissors jump (feet over the bar first).

Jean Shiley, the winner; Babe
Didrikson, second; and Eva Dawes
of Canada, third in the high jump.

Babe Didrikson clears the same height as Jean Shiley. She
was given second place. It was decided that her technique
was illegal (head over the bar first), even though she had
been jumping that way throughout the entire competition.

113

7.
Did England Really Win the World Cup?

THOSE WHO HAVE SEEN QUEEN ELIZABETH II OF EN-
gland show any excitement in public are members of the most
exclusive club in the world. Nevertheless, a privileged few saw
just that on the afternoon of July 30, 1966, at Wembly
Stadium in London. A few seconds before the end of the
World Cup final, with England about to defeat West Germany
4–2, the queen clasped her hands tightly and whispered to an
aide: "*When* will it be over?"

All things are relative, but Her Majesty's break with her
traditional calm was comparable to the howling of millions of
men, women, and children in the British Isles who laughed,
cried, danced in the streets, and sang throughout the night as
their beloved English team won the twelve-inch gold cup
symbolic of world supremacy in soccer. After the victory,
thousands of delirious Britains chanted: "England, England,
England" in uproars that could be compared to the VE-Day
celebrations twenty-one years before.

It did not matter that the victory was tainted because of a
decisive goal in overtime that to this day remains one of the
most controversial moments in the history of the World Cup.
All that counted was that the World Cup belonged to England.

But now, years later, the debate will be revived anew, for
"instant replay" frame-by frame photographs are being
printed for the first time. Depending on where one's loyalties
lie, England's winning goal remains the most arguable split
second of any sport moment in history.

The World Cup final of 1966 was no ordinary contest. To the sports world outside the United States, the World Cup is the Super Bowl, World Series, and Olympic Games rolled into one—a two-year elimination contest that begins with some seventy countries battling it out for the sixteen final places.

World Cup fever has no comparable atmosphere in any international sport. The fact that soccer is The Game in every hemisphere of the world gives it an unequaled following. The length of the elimination contests that led to the final game kept World Cup news continually on the television screens and in the press.

When this long process climaxes into victory and defeat measured in the infinitesimal part of a second of the final game, it must remain as *the* most controversial moment in sports.

England and West Germany reached that momentous split second by coming through victoriously in the final sixteen-team elimination round. The sixteen finalists were divided into four groups. Each team played the other three teams in its group a single game in a round-robin series. Two points were given for a victory, and one point for a tie. The two teams with the most points in each group advanced to the eight-team quarterfinals.

England and Uruguay qualified in Group 1 while West Germany and Argentina advanced from Group 2. The real shocks came from the results of the other two group eliminations.

Brazil, favored by most to win the Cup, was eliminated due mainly to the below-par performance of their revered Pele, who played with severe injuries received in Brazil's first game of the final series. Portugal and Hungary advanced from the group that saw Brazil's elimination.

Group 4 had its comparable disaster. Third-favorite Italy was beaten by the little-known North Korean team as well as the Soviet Union. The Italians had to sneak back home in disgrace.

England, West Germany, Portugal, and the Soviet Union then moved into the semifinals with victories as Argentina, Uruguay, North Korea, and Hungary fell by the wayside. England then beat Portugal 2–1 in its semifinal, and West Germany advanced with a 2–1 victory over the Soviet Union.

The long wait was at last over. England would meet West Germany for the World Cup.

More than one World Cup had been won and lost by the luck of the draw, and up to the final game, the English team had drawn nothing but horseshoes. First, they were fortunate enough to have drawn the easiest opening qualifying group. In their three-game round-robin series they advanced to the quarterfinals without having a goal scored against them. Then they had been saved the possibility of a grueling semifinal match when Italy and Brazil, both pretourney favorites, were knocked out in the qualifying round. Finally, they were the host nation with a roaring home crowd of almost 100,000 fans urging them on against a West German team that had never beaten them in an international match.

These solid advantages suddenly turned sour to the lovers of England's historic soccer tradition. When the two teams trotted onto the hallowed Wembly pitch, there for all to see was the English team wearing red. Instead of their traditional white shirts, a red-shirted English team would do battle against a white-shirted West German eleven. For years during international matches, the chorus of England's supporters would sing throughout the afternoon, ''The Whites Go Marching In,'' to the tune of ''The Saints Go Marching In.'' ''Simple solution,'' Charlie Chan used to say, and the British fans had it. ''The Reds Go Marching In'' echoed throughout Wembly the entire afternoon.

England lost the coin toss. The West Germans scored first and aside from the practical advantage of having a 1−0 lead, the goal had important psychological overtones. The invincibility of England's goalkeeper, Gordon Banks, had been questioned. When Helmut Haller of West Germany kicked one past Banks at the ten-minute mark of the opening half, it marked the first time that Banks had given up a goal from the field in the whole of the final eliminations. Banks had gone through its opening three-game round-robin series against Uruguay, Mexico, and France without giving up a goal. When England defeated Argentina in the quarterfinals 1−0, goalkeeper Banks' perfect record was still intact. In defeating Portugal 2−1 in the semifinals, Banks was finally scored upon. But this was on a penalty shot at point-blank range by Portugal's high-scoring star, Eusebio. For the uninitiated, Banks had to defend a 24-foot-wide, 8-foot-high cage alone, with no defensive men to help him. Eusebio scored easily from twelve yards out.

Now, in the last round, England, which had advanced to the finals with its iron clad defense, had been scored on first.

For the moment the situation seemed serious. In all its previous final World Cup contests, England had not scored more than two goals in any one game.

However, six minutes after Haller's score, Geoffry Hurst tied up the game with a header past the West German goalkeeper, Hans Tilkowski. There was no further scoring in the first half, and the teams left the field with the score 1−1. After a ten-minute intermission, the teams returned for the final forty-five minutes of regulation play.

England confidently believed that another goal would give them the Cup. Their previous game plans had worked out that way—two goals and hold. With twelve minutes left to play in the game, they got it. Martin Peters put one past Tilkowski, and England was ahead 2−1. As the minutes ticked off, the crowd roar swelled in anticipation of victory. "The Reds Go Marching In" was sung and resung.

Then, with less than a minute to play, Wolfgang Weber of West Germany slammed one past Banks, and the game was tied 2−2. The game would now go into overtime. Unlike overtime games in the United States, this was no "sudden death" affair. Two fifteen-minute periods would be played.

At the ten-minute mark, the most controversial play in World Cup history took place.

England had control of the ball in an offensive zone, and three of its greatest heroes would be involved. Nobby Stiles, the smallest player on both teams, had control of the ball and edged it up to Alan Ball. Ball sent it off to his right where Geoffry Hurst had one step on his defender. From his position some twenty-one feet to the right of the goal, Hurst let loose a thunderous right-footed kick, head high and straight at goalkeeper Tilkowski. Tilkowski, already braced, tried to catch or deflect the kick, but Hurst's drive was too powerful. Tilkowski got his hands in front of his face, and the ball caromed off.

Only by stopping the film in frame-by-frame sequence is it possible to determine what happened in exactly 3/24 of a second. When the ball hit Tilkowski's hands the momentum sent the ball upward and behind him. Careful measurements clearly prove that the ball hit Tilkowski's protecting hands when it was five feet off the ground.

The ball, 1/24 of a second after the Tilkowski deflection, is seen hitting the top crossbar, which is eight feet off the ground. The ball then dropped straight down on what appears from the camera angle to land on the white goal line.

117

Geoffrey Hurst of Great
Britain is about to kick the ball
toward the West German
goal. Hans Tilkowski, the
West German goalie, has
clear view of the play in front
of him.

Tilkowski braces for the shot.
He has moved into a
semicrouch. Meanwhile,
Hurst's momentum sends him
to the turf.

Tilkowski blocks the ball
with his hands.

118

The ball bounces high and behind him. It then caroms off the top crossbar.

The ball bounces straight down.

Medium shot of the ball hitting the goal line.

119

Blown-up frame of film showing the ball at the goal line.

A larger blow-up of the ball and the goal line. Soccer rules state that "the whole of the ball" must pass over the line for a goal.

The ball (arrow) bounces up again, away from the mouth of the goal. Note that no official is within reasonable viewing range of the incident.

A British player signals a goal as a West German alongside him prepares to "head" the ball out of harm's way.

121

The ball is on the white line for exactly one frame again—1/24 of a second. Then, because of the momentum of the original Hurst kick, the Tilkowski deflection, and the hitting of the top crossbar, severe reverse spin sent the ball bounding out to the playing field where a German player is seen "heading" it over the goal line, out of harm's way.

Soccer rules state: "A goal is scored when the *whole of the ball* has passed over the goal line." The Swiss referee, Gottfried Dienst, was in no position to see where the ball landed. Official rules dictate that he call on a linesman to make the decision. The closest linesman to the action was Tofik Bahkramov, a Russian. The frame-by-frame photos show that Bahkramov was stationed some forty yards from the goal, on a slight angle to the left of the cage. More important, from that distance it would be next to impossible to make anything but a guess, since the ball was on the ground for only 1/24 of a second.

In effect, the World Cup was decided by a "visual impression," with more than one West German fan sarcastically commenting that Bahkramov automatically called it a goal because it was kicked by a player wearing a red shirt.

The West Germans protested vehemently, but as in all sports, judgment calls are never reversed.

There was still plenty of time left in overtime play for West Germany to come back, but England was not about to let the West Germans off the hook again. West Germany was forced to attack without regard to defense, and it was almost a foregone conclusion that England would score again. Just before the game ended, Geoffry Hurst scored his third goal of the afternoon. England had the World Cup by the score of 4–2.

So England had the 1966 World Cup. Eight years later, in 1974, West Germany worked its way again into the final. This time, there were no mishaps and no red shirts. The German team beat the Netherlands and at long last were the owners of the most coveted trophy in sport—the World Cup.

8.
The
Dirty
Derby

THE WORST SPORTS MOVIES EVER MADE WERE those Hollywood horse-racing epics of the 1930s and '40s. Invariably the film would end with the bad jockey, usually played by a fine character actor named Frankie Darrow, bashing the skull of the good jockey, portrayed by someone like Mickey Rooney, for what seemed like a ten-minute boxing bout down the homestretch. Finally, Rooney would cluck into his mount's ear, and the horse would jet-propel past the thrashing whip of Darrow to victory, thereby saving the mortgaged ranch for someone like Walter Brennan.

The 1933 Kentucky Derby was probably the original story line for all this Hollywood fiction. It was there that two jockeys displayed their punching ability down the homestretch and turned this derby into the wildest chase in the history of the classic.

The two jockeys involved were Don Meade aboard Broker's Tip and Herb Fisher riding Head Play. Meade was known as one of the roughest riders in racing history, but surprisingly the visual evidence indicates that his participation in the 1933 Derby fracas was more in the form of retaliation than as an initiator. Yet in subsequent years Meade was all but run out of racing for his abusive behavior both on and off the track.

Meade's mount, Broker's Tip, was owned by the revered Colonel E. R. Bradley, and this association probably played a

Don Meade aboard Broker's Tip (No. 16; closest to the rail) and Herb Fisher riding Head Play (No. 9) battle down to the wire in the 1933 Kentucky Derby.

strong part in the final decision giving Broker's Tip the victory. Colonel Bradley's horses had won three previous Derbys, but Broker's Tip seemed an unlikely choice for the then unprecedented fourth win. Broker's Tip had not won a race before the Derby and should not have had much play in the betting. So strong was the prestige of Colonel Bradley, however, that Broker's Tip went to the post as an inflated 8–1 shot.

The favorites in the race were the W. R. Coe entry of Ladysman and Pomponius. When Colonel Bradley scratched his highly rated Boilermaker the night before the race, most experts believed he had lost his big chance for the top prize. Incidentally, the superstitious Bradley named all his horses with names starting with the letter *B*. His other Derby winners were Behave Yourself in 1921, Bubbling Over in 1926, and Burgoo King in 1932.

By today's racing codes, Charley O. should have won the 1933 Derby. Charley O. finished third, some five lengths behind Broker's Tip and Head Play, the two horses involved in

the controversy. But "instant replay" of the race now provides conclusive evidence that both Meade and Fisher's antics should have disqualified both their mounts.

The year 1933 was thirteen years before patrol-judge films came into use and five years before the photo finish decided close finishes. Nevertheless, films of the race were taken by a newsreel company. Slowing them down to frame-by-frame action, the Meade-Fisher confrontation comes alive.

Even to the naked eyes of the judges, there was something amiss. Both jockeys were suspended for thirty days, but the setdown proved more hurtful to Fisher than to Meade. He not only lost the Derby but also missed riding Head Play in the Preakness. Head Play won the Preakness while Broker's Tip finished tenth.

The Derby was uneventful until the stretch run. Fisher got Head Play off well and moved him into the lead at the half-mile pole. At that point Broker's Tip was ninth in a thirteen-horse field. As the horses came off the final turn, Head Play and Charley O. were battling for the lead.

Fisher driving Meade's mount closer to the rail.

125

Head-on photograph of the finish shows Fisher (on the left)
and Meade fighting each other.

Broker's Tip is first to cross the finish line. Herb Fisher stands up in his stirrups and continues to battle.

Saving ground on the inside, Meade took Broker's Tip past tiring horses into third place. Rounding the final turn, Broker's Tip was a length behind the leaders. Coming off the turn, Meade took a bold chance. He cut the corner with his mount, taking the inside position closest to the rail but away from the heavy footing on the very inside of the track. In the middle of the stretch, Charley O. fell back and Meade took Broker's Tip nose to nose with Head Play, who was outside him.

Both Fisher and Meade were whipping their mounts, but about halfway down the stretch, Head Play slowly began to move inside, crowding Meade and Broker's Tip. Meade, feeling the pressure, and not wishing to get any closer to the rail where the footing was heavy, grabbed Head Play's saddle-cloth, trying to keep him away.

127

Fisher said afterward, "I felt like I was draggin' the other horse a quarter of a mile."

With Meade holding on to Head Play's saddlecloth, Fisher leaned over, trying to push Meade off.

Forty years later Meade said, "He was trying to hold me with one hand and hit me with the other, with the whip. At one point he didn't even have hold of his reins."

Meade had a strong hold on Broker's Tip, but the duel evidently had little effect on his ride down the stretch. Broker's Tip won by a nose.

Most of the 40,000 hysterical spectators missed the infighting. All they saw were two horses pounding toward the finish line with both jockeys flailing away with their whips. From the stands it seemed like a typical head-to-head finish with both jocks trying to get the best out of their mounts. The spectators got their first inkling that something was wrong a few yards past the finish line when Herb Fisher stood up in his stirrups and began whacking Meade with his whip. Then Fisher dismounted and ran to the stewards with his protest. The claim was disallowed, and Broker's Tip remained a nose victor.

Now, more than four decades later, Meade has mellowed from the hard-riding, hard-talking jock that made him countless enemies both on and off the track. "I think if it were any other race but the Derby and I was riding for anyone else but Colonel Bradley, they would have taken me down," he says today.

Because of Colonel Bradley, the Broker's Tip victory was popular with the crowd. But when Meade returned to the jockeys' quarters after the victory ceremonies, he was met by a sobbing Fisher. Fisher went after Meade with a bootjack, a hard leather pole. They were separated by other jockeys before any damage could be done. Fisher received an extra five days' suspension to go with the original thirty days for rough riding.

Meade went on to become one of America's great jockeys, winning the national crown in 1939 and again in 1941. Fisher, riding mostly out of Chicago, never did gain national prominence, other than the publicity he received in the 1933 Derby.

For thirty-two years the jockeys never spoke. In 1965 there came a Hollywood ending to what was then an unfinished script. A dinner was held at the Pimlico Race Track to honor Jackie Westrope, who was being inducted into the Jockey Hall of Fame. Both Meade and Fisher attended. They

Long shot of Broker's Tip defeating Head Play.

avoided each other as they had in the past. Then one of those spontaneous dramatic moments took place that would not be believed if it happened in a movie. Sonny Workman, another famous jockey of the era, who ironically finished fourth aboard Ladysman in the 1933 Derby, noticed that Meade and Fisher were standing within a few feet of each other.

Workman turned Meade toward Fisher and said, "It's time you two made up." Fisher and Meade stared at each other. Then they shook hands.

As if on a given signal, the orchestra began to play. Fisher smiled at Meade, then asked Meade's wife to dance. It was a classy real-life ending to a bad Hollywood movie.

129

Close-up of the finish at close quarters.

Herb Fisher's protest was
disallowed. Don Meade on Broker's
Tip is in the winner's circle.

9.
The Tragic Birthdays of Rocky Marciano and Carmine Vingo

IF CARMINE VINGO HAD DIED TWENTY-SEVEN YEARS ago, Rocky Marciano probably would be alive today. But that's like saying that John F. Kennedy would still be the senator from Massachusetts if 8,858 Illinois and 22,091 New Jersey voters had gone for Nixon instead of Kennedy in the 1960 presidential election. The slim Illinois and New Jersey margins gave Kennedy the victory, and with it, his rendezvous with death in a Dallas motorcade three years later.

Carmine Vingo lived, and because he did, Rocky Marciano went on to become heavyweight champion of the world, only to keep his appointment with tragedy while en route home from one of the many public appearances he was called on to make more than a decade after retiring from the ring as undefeated heavyweight champion of the world.

December 30, 1949, was a painfully cold day in New York. The temperature was hovering near zero, and Madison Square Garden was a little more than half filled for the weekly Friday-night fight card. Three ten-rounders were the featured bouts of the evening. The first of the main events was a scheduled ten-rounder between Rocky Marciano of Brockton, Massachusetts, and Carmine Vingo of the Bronx, New York.

The twenty-six-year-old Marciano had an unblemished record. He had KO'd 23 of 25 opponents, and had won decisions in the other two fights. Vingo, a twenty-year-old, 189-pound slugger, was a 3−1 underdog. Yet some "smart" Stillman's Gym money was, surprisingly, on the underdog.

Vingo was on a twelve-bout winning streak, and he was being billed as a younger Marciano. To his supporters, the odds were an attractive overlay. In fact, some of the less timid were predicting that a Vingo win over Marciano was the first step to the heavyweight title, discounting Rocky's record as the usual out-of-town fluff manufactured to set up a big gate.

Vingo, too, was sure of himself. The day before the fight, December 29, was his birthday, but he had postponed festivities until after the fight. He was certain there would be cause for a threefold celebration—his win over Marciano, his birthday, and his upcoming March marriage to Kitty Rea.

At 180 pounds, Marciano was outweighed by Vingo, but at the opening bell he tore into Vingo with a ferocious two-fisted attack. Marciano swarmed all over his heavier opponent, but this type of brawl was the only style Vingo knew. He stood toe to toe with Marciano, giving as much as he took.

At the halfway mark of the opening round, Marciano landed a smashing left hook to the jaw, the same punch that would knock out Jersey Joe Walcott three years later and win Marciano the heavyweight crown. Vingo went down for a nine count. Marciano swarmed in again, but Vingo crashed over a thunderous right to the jaw; Marciano staggered and was rubbery legged. His knees buckled, but he weathered the round. At the bell it was all Vingo.

The second round was a carbon copy of the opening stanza. They again stood at point-blank range, flailing away with blockbusters that had the crowd roaring and on its feet. The third, fourth, and fifth rounds were duplications of the first two, as both men forgot about defense and just threw leather. The only certain thing was that one or the other had to go down soon.

Vingo was taking an unusual amount of punishment around the head; in turn, he was rocking Marciano's jaw and midsection with equal fury.

The sixth round got under way, and though Marciano was slightly ahead on points, Vingo seemed to have lost none of his steam. At this point, Vingo's supporters had only one concern. This was his first ten-rounder, and there were doubts as to whether he could stand up over the full distance. Nothing occurred during the first minute of the sixth round, however, that indicated their man would give ground first.

Suddenly, a little past the minute mark, Vingo's face showed the pained expression of a fighter whose arms were leaden and whose legs were entwined in heavy weights.

133

Carmine Vingo (left) blocks a Rocky Marciano right-hand to the head.
The two fighters stood toe-to-toe for five rounds, exchanging blows.

Referee Harry Ebbets
motions Rocky Marciano to a
neutral corner before starting
to count Vingo out.

With the ten counts
completed, Referee Ebbets
goes to the aid of Vingo.

135

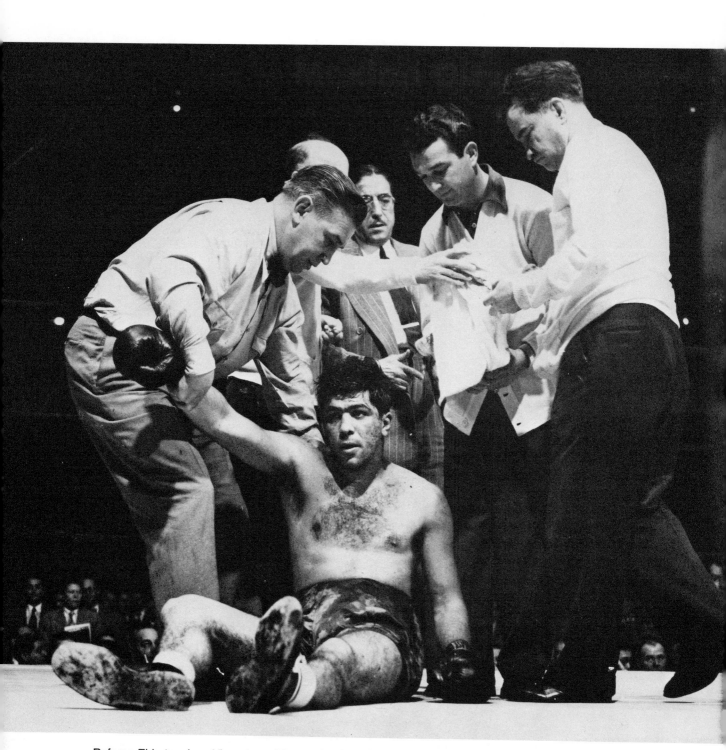

Referee Ebbets raises Vingo to a sitting position, as his handlers watch. Dr. Vincent Nardiello, the Boxing Commission physician (wearing glasses), rushes into the ring.

Vingo's mouth was open, and he was breathing hard. He looked not unlike the way he had looked earlier in the bout, but his arms and legs were not responding.

Marciano let loose with a tremendous left hook that caught Vingo flush on the jaw, and the tired battler slowly crumpled to the canvas. There was no need for referee Harry Ebbets to count. Vingo was out cold. Vingo's corner man, manager Jackie Levine, and trainers Whitey Bimstein and Freddie Brown, three of the best and most respected men in the fight game, rushed into the ring to assist their fallen fighter.

Almost immediately after them, Vincent Nardiello, the Boxing Commission physician, jumped into the ring from his front-row seat. Dr. Nardiello worked over Vingo for a few minutes, then he called for a stretcher. Marciano, happily receiving the congratulations of his handlers, suddenly turned somber, looking frightened as Vingo remained still. Vingo was carried to his dressing room as Nardiello summoned the aid of his assistant, Russell Kimball. Finally, Nardiello called for an ambulance.

Vingo is placed on a stretcher. Unable to get an ambulance, Dr. Nardiello (right) ordered that he be wrapped in blankets and carried a few blocks to St. Claire's Hospital.

Twenty minutes went by, and the ambulance failed to arrive. Word was received that the two ambulances from St. Claire's Hospital were out on emergency calls. Nardiello couldn't wait. He ordered that Vingo be wrapped up in blankets and carried on a stretcher to St. Claire's Hospital, two blocks away. Vingo was lying unconscious as his aides began to pile blankets over him. Someone mentioned that the temperature was near zero, so several of Vingo's friends took off their overcoats and lay them over the blankets.

As Vingo lay there awaiting an eight-man team of special police that would carry him through the frozen Manhattan streets, Reverend Paul Gallivan of Boston, a spectator at the fight, gave the last rites of the Catholic church to Vingo. Several of the fighter's coatless friends were now weeping.

Vingo was carried out of the Fiftieth Street exit of Madison Square Garden. Onlookers outside stared incredulously as the eight stretcher-bearers mince-stepped down the icy street toward Tenth Avenue and Fifty-first Street where St. Claire's Hospital was located. Rumors spread through Madison Square Garden that Vingo was dead, and some reporters began writing leads comparing this night to the one sixteen years before when Ernie Shaaf had died after being knocked out by the giant Primo Carnera.

Vingo was not dead, but his condition was critical. Shortly after midnight, Dr. Nardiello reported that X rays revealed that Vingo suffered a concussion of the brain, "contusions and lacerations of the brain." Vingo's left side was paralyzed. Vingo regained consciousness about an hour after arriving at the hospital, but intermittently lapsed into a coma. He was placed on the critical list, and Nardiello announced that Vingo had a 50–50 chance of surviving.

Vingo's father, brother, and sister stood vigil; from time to time, they were let into the room. When Vingo regained occasional consciousness, he showed some recognition with his eyes, but he couldn't speak. Michael Vingo, Carmine's father, amazed reporters with what had to be fearful bravado. He said that he was certain his son could beat Marciano in a return bout.

Marciano delayed his return trip to his home in Brockton, Massachusetts, and visited the hospital on Saturday night, New Year's Eve. Sitting outside Vingo's room, Marciano was a forlorn figure. From time to time he lowered his head into his hands. After a few minutes, he responded to reporters' questions with tear-filled eyes. Finally, he answered the question that was in every reporter's mind but was never asked.

"This is it," Marciano said slowly. "If he doesn't make it, I'm through."

Dr. Nardiello put his arms around Marciano and told him that Vingo would be in critical condition for at least two weeks and that he would keep in close touch. If there was any change in Vingo's condition, he would let Marciano know. Marciano returned to his home.

Two weeks later, Vingo was out of danger. His left side was still paralyzed, and he was blind in his left eye. With therapy, the paralysis slowly receded. But today Vingo is still blind in one eye and has only partial vision in the other.

Marciano contributed his $1,500 purse, plus an additional $500, toward Vingo's hospital expenses. A year after the fight, Rocky invited Vingo and Kitty, now married, to his own wedding. Less than two years after the Vingo fight, Marciano knocked out Joe Louis in the eighth round, setting the scene for his thirteenth-round knockout of Jersey Joe Walcott for the heavyweight championship title on September 23, 1952. Marciano retired undefeated in 1956 but continued to be in demand for public appearances throughout the country. On August 31, 1969, he was killed in the crash of a light plane while returning from a speaking engagement in Iowa.

At their home in Brockton, Marciano's wife received the news as she was making preparations for his forty-sixth birthday party the following day. Ironically, twenty years earlier, his smashing fists were responsible for the cancellation of another birthday celebration—the twentieth birthday of Carmine Vingo.

10.
How Jim Ryun Lost Immortality in Mexico City

FRANCESCO ARESE OF ITALY IS NOT ONE OF THE most familiar names on the roster of great 1,500-meter racers in track history, but when the *Rise and Fall of Jim Ryun* story is written, Arese's name will hold a prominent place as the runner who started Ryun's demise. The ironic part of Arese's contribution to the downfall of the great American runner was the fact that Ryun was not even in the race.

Ryun's high and low points have been mostly associated with three dramatic races he had with Kip Keino of Kenya. The Ryun-Keino saga began on July 8, 1967, in Los Angeles, when Ryun set a world record for the 1,500-meter run with a 3.33.1 clocking. Keino was one of the victims of Ryun's amazing performance.

The world record made Ryun a pre-Mexico City Olympics favorite to become the first U.S. miler to win the event since Mel Shepard's London victory in 1908. Ryun lost to Keino in the final, however, trailing the Kenyan marvel by some twenty-five yards at the finish line.

Four years later, at the Munich Olympics, Ryun had a disastrous fall in a preliminary heat and failed to qualify for the final. Ironically, Keino won the heat in which Ryun fell and then went on to win the silver medal behind Finland's Pekka Vasala's smashing ''come from behind'' victory in the final.

Surrounding Ryun's three crucial races with Keino was a career that included three Olympic teams, injuries, world records, illness, emotional problems, an allergy—but no gold medals.

Now how does Francesco Arese fit into the Ryun story of victory and defeat? This Italian 1,500-meter internationalist was the second best miler in the world during 1970 and 1971 but was unfortunately an innocent contributor to the greatest con game that ever took place in the history of Olympic 1,500-meter competition.

To set the scene properly, we have to turn the clock back to October 18, 1968, a Friday, for the qualifying rounds of the 1,500-meter run at the Mexico City stadium. Olympic rules dictate that every nation can enter a representative in each event, even though the athlete may not be of international caliber. Consequently, qualifying heats are staged to cut down the field. Five heats were scheduled, with the first five finishers in each heat moving into the semifinals to be held the following day. Kip Keino won the first heat easily, and his victory was duplicated in the third heat by his teammate, Ben Jipcho.

The twenty-one-year-old Ryun was already an Olympic veteran as he toed the mark for the fourth heat. Four years before, as a schoolboy sensation, Ryun had finished ninth in the semifinal in Tokyo and was eliminated from the final by New Zealand's great Peter Snell. Between Tokyo and Mexico City, however, Ryun set the world record for the 1,500-meter distance and was now considered the favorite to win the gold medal.

Munich, 1972: Jim Ryun, in next-to-last place, and Ghana's Billy Fordjour, in last place, fall to the ground after their legs got tangled up, in the fourth heat of the 1,500-meter race.

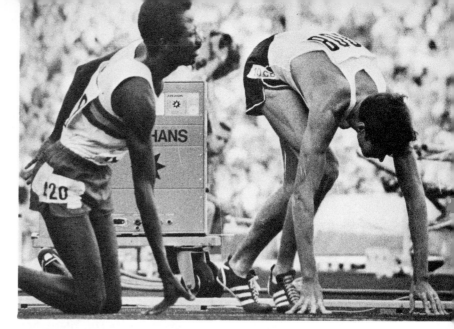

Ryun gets up and finishes the race,
coming in ninth in a field of ten.

Kip Keino, winner of the heat, consoles his longtime rival Ryun.

Ryun gave his supporters no concern as he turned in the best time of the day in his heat, just a little more than twelve seconds off his world record. It was a sparkling time for a qualifying race, and Ryun finished well under wraps and in good physical condition.

Ryun's postrace condition was important. To win the gold medal he would have to run the 1,500-meter distance on three successive days, and he knew only too well the terrible scenes

143

that took place on previous days in the 10,000- and 5,000-meter runs. Internationalists by the score fell prostrate to the track, victims of the tortuous 7,350-foot altitude of Mexico City.

Keino's problem was even greater than Ryun's. The Kenyan workhorse had competed in the 10,000 meters and two heats of the 5,000 meters, winning the silver medal in the 5,000 when he was just beaten to the finish by Mohamed Gammoudi of Tunisia.

By the luck of the draw, Ryun and Keino found themselves in the second semifinal heat. But the first semifinal must have held more than just casual interest to Kip Keino, based on what transpired the following day in the final. In that race were seven world-class 1,500-meter runners. Only the first six finishers would qualify for the next day's final. They were Bodo Tummler and Harald Norpoth of West Germany, Jacques Boxberger of France, Tom Von Ruden of the United States, Henry Szordykowski of Poland, Francesco Arese of Italy, and Ben Jipcho of Kenya. Five other starters rounded out the twelve-man semifinal heat, but they were not given much of a chance to qualify. In effect, seven men were racing for six qualifying positions.

The finish of the first semifinal was incredible. The last 200 meters was run as if it were the final. Down the straightaway they came, with just a few yards separating the first seven runners. As they crossed the finish line, it was evident that Bodo Tummler of West Germany had won, followed by Jacques Boxberger of France. But five other men finished under the proverbial "blanket," with four qualifying spots left.

After a few moments the results were flashed on the electric scoreboard. Following Tummler and Boxberger were Tom Von Ruden of the United States in third, Szordykowski of Poland fourth, Norpoth of West Germany fifth, Ben Jipcho of Kenya sixth, and Francesco Arese of Italy seventh. Jipcho had beaten Francesco Arese of Italy by two-tenths of a second for the sixth and last qualifying position.

In the second semifinal, Ryun gave confidence to his supporters with a five-yard victory over Keino. In typical Ryun fashion he stayed off the pace until the final turn, then made his move. As he neared the finish he twice looked around at the second-place Keino, who seemed content merely to qualify. Ryun's semifinal time was 3.51.2, some seven seconds slower than his qualifying-round victory and more than eighteen seconds off his world record.

Sunday, September 20, the twelve finalists lined up for the 1,500-meter final. Joining Ryun for the United States were Tom Von Ruden and Marty Liquori. Kip Keino and Ben Jipcho represented Kenya.

The gun sounded. Jipcho sprang from the starting line as if he were running 800 meters instead of the metric mile. He sprinted to the front in a mad dash that gave credibility to the words that Neil Amdur, who then was the track analyst for the *New York Times*, wrote after the semifinals:

> Kenya has two runners in the final. Kipchoge Keino and B. W. Jipcho, and there is some speculation that the Kenyans may send out a tactical "rabbit"—possibly Jipcho—to set a strong early pace and keep Ryun from laying back until the last lap.

Jipcho turned in a 56-second 400 meters, some 12 seconds faster than both semifinal heats of the day before. Keino loped contentedly back in the pack, with Ryun staying in sight of him. Ryun knew that Jipcho's pace was a killing one but assumed that if he stayed close to Keino, he would still have enough left to win a stretch duel with his strong finishing kick.

As Jipcho finished his blazing 400 meters, Keino, from his position back in the pack, made a mad dash around the field and tore by his teammate as if he, too, had gone mad. The race was less than half over, but in retrospect the Kenyan strategy is now fully apparent. Quite simply, the plan was to confuse Ryun early in the race and make the American miler commit himself to changing his race plan.

Ryun had two choices. He could either take Keino's bait and move up with him, which would have taken away from his finishing kick, or he could conserve his strength hoping that Keino could not keep up the pace.

As they moved into the next-to-last lap, Keino seemed as strong as when he began his initial spurt. Now Ryun was worried that Keino would "steal" the race, and he made his move earlier than planned. He started after Keino, still trying to keep something in reserve for the final kick.

But Jipcho and Keino had done their work well. Ryun was gaining feet, but not yards. Keino was coming back to Ryun but not fast enough. When Keino crossed the finish line, he was still some twenty-five yards in front of the world record holder.

A few yards past the finish line, Keino was joined by Jipcho. The two men ran a victory lap arm in arm as the crowd cheered. The next day, the press of the world wrote of the "dual victory" of Keino and Jipcho, even though Jipcho had predictably faded to a tenth-place finish in a field of twelve.

Since the race, Keino persistently denied that there was any prerace strategy involved. It nevertheless is historical fact that the final was run in a manner unlike any of the previous races of the competition, and it was the *only* 1,500-meter race in Mexico City in which the two men appeared.

Even though Keino and Jipcho trotted arm in arm around the Mexico City track after Keino's victory, it was well known that Jipcho was upset with Keino's postrace comments. Or rather, his lack of comment. Rumors circulated through the Olympic Village that the Kenyan Olympic Committee had decided to "sacrifice" Jipcho at the expense of their national hero. This fact was later confirmed by a Kenyan track official; Jipcho was indeed asked to sacrifice himself.

Jipcho readily went along with the idea but felt slighted that Keino never publicly acknowledged his contribution. To this day, Jipcho bristles whenever the race is brought up. He says, "Our plan was unfair to people like Jim Ryun and probably to me, too. I feel that Jim Ryun would have won a gold medal, but because of the whole thing, it destroyed almost everybody. It was very good for Kenya, very good, but it was unfair to the other guys."

When Jim Ryun recently retired, every news story told of his troubles dating back to the 1968 Mexico City finals when he lost to Kip Keino. One wonders if Jim Ryun's career would have turned out differently if Francesco Arese had beaten Ben Jipcho out of the last qualifying spot for the 1,500-meter final.

Ben Jipcho (No. 564) of Kenya bursts out into the lead with a blistering opening lap. Kip Keino, partially hidden in the rear, knows that Jipcho is the "rabbit." Jim Ryun, also hidden, is alongside Keino.

At 800 meters, Kip Keino makes his own sprint
and goes 20 meters into the lead.

Coming off the final turn, Keino leads Ryun.

Keino wins. Ryun is second.

Ben Jipcho, the "rabbit," and winner
Kip Keino take a victory lap.

11.
Spiridon Louis, "Savior of the Olympic Games"

THE MARATHON RUN IS THE MOST HISTORIC EVENT in the Olympic program. When the Games were revived in Athens in 1896, the marathon was included as a remembrance of the past glory of Greece. It was scheduled to be the last event of the seven-day Athens Olympiad. No one knew, at the time, that the event would have a far greater impact than as a historical reminder of Ancient Greece. The marathon run, in fact, "saved" the Olympic Games from going into extinction.

The history behind the marathon run is etched in the culture of Greece. On the morning of September 5, in the year 490 B.C., an invading Persian army of 20,000 troops awaited orders to attack. A little more than a mile away, in full view of the Persian army, stood some 7,000 Greek warriors.

The Greeks had marched from Athens to the Plains of Marathon a few days earlier. Now, on this small coastal flatland that overlooks the Bay of Marathon, the battle would take place. It would decide the fate of Greece—and as historians later pointed out, it "decided the fate of Western civilization."

Heroically, the Greek defenders repulsed the Persian attack, losing less than 200 men. The Persians, in complete rout, left more than 6,000 dead on the battlefield of the Plains of Marathon.

Nearly twenty-five hundred years have passed since the Battle of Marathon, and many legends have evolved from the momentous Greek victory. The most famous story of the battle was the event that took place immediately after it—the run of the famed warrior Pheidippides from Marathon to Athens with news of the great Greek triumph. Over the centuries, history books have dramatically recounted the run of Pheidippides, which ended with his arrival in Athens. He proclaimed: "Rejoice, we conquer." Then he dropped dead from exhaustion.

The story is correct except for two major points. The runner was not Pheidippides, and the warrior who did make the epic journey did not say, "Rejoice, we conquer."

Through the centuries since the battle, romantic historians have added to Herodotus' account of the battle some Hollywood embellishments. For some strange reason, Pheidippides has always been mentioned by Western writers as the warrior who ran to Athens with the glad tidings. Yet even the smallest Greek schoolboy would know it was impossible for Pheidippides to have made the run. Pheidippides had just completed a 150-mile round-trip run to Sparta in an attempt to enlist the aid of the Spartans, the Athenians' natural enemy, for a common Greek defense against the Persian invaders.

The historian Herodotus made no mention of the unknown warrior who ran the glorious distance from Marathon to Athens, but the runner's words have been recorded: *"Ne nikhkamen."* Western writers have translated the Greek words as "Rejoice, we conquer." The actual translation is: "Yes, we are victorious."

It matters little that these bits of historical fact have been recorded inaccurately. More important is the little-known fact that the run from Marathon to Athens climaxed a victory that perhaps saved Western civilization as we know it today, and also saved the modern Olympics from fading into oblivion.

In 1896, Greece, because of its historical association with the Olympian theme, was voted the host nation for the first modern revival of the Games. Historically and emotionally, there could have been no other choice. From the practical standpoint, no selection could have been worse.

Greece in 1896 was beset with financial problems. The treasury was empty, and most of the population was impoverished and starving. Only a last-minute gift of a million drachmas from a Greek merchant, George Averoff, made it possible for a beautiful marble stadium to rise at the site where the unknown warrior made his famous proclamation more than two thousand years before.

The first modern Olympics was a sort of catch-as-catch-can affair. There were no formal national teams, but there were representatives from nine countries: Greece, United States, Great Britain, France, Germany, Denmark, Hungary, Switzerland, and Australia. The national pride of Greece was at stake; as the host nation, they entered more athletes than all the other countries combined.

The Opening Day ceremonies were glorious, and on the following day more than 70,000 fans, predominately Greek, settled in their seats for the actual competition. Greek athletes won nothing. Disaster followed disaster as United States athletes won nine of the eleven events contested over the first four days. Great Britain won the other two. The Greek athletes won not one event, and the fans in the stands came alive with the 1896 version of "Yankee go home."

On the final day, with Greek newspapers blasting the professionalism of the Americans and calling for an end to this athletic farce, the Marathon race was scheduled to close the games. A final honor for Greece's Olympian heritage.

The race began on the Plains of Marathon, at the precise spot where Greek defenders repulsed the Persians in 490 B.C. At each kilometer couriers on horseback galloped ahead to the stadium with news of the runners leading in the race.

As the fans in the Olympic stadium waited, they saw men on horseback gallop into the stadium at various intervals and rush to the Royal Box where Prince Constantine and Prince George of Greece were seated. There, a whispered message was given to the princes. From their response, it was obvious that the news was not good.

At various times throughout the afternoon, runners from the United States, Great Britain, Germany, and Hungary led. But as the time for the first runners to arrive at the stadium approached, an excited horseman entered the stadium at full gallop and made his way to the Royal Box. The 70,000 fans leaned forward and watched for a sign. First it started as a whisper, then it became a roar. Word had been received that a Greek runner had been spotted on the approaches to the stadium and that no one was in front of him.

Minutes went by, and then it happened. Into the stadium came the Greek runner, a shepherd named Spiridon Louis. He was exhausted but slowly made his way down the straightaway toward the finish line. The crowd exploded, and the emotional outburst urged the shepherd onward.

152

Prince George and Prince Constantine leaped from their box to the track and formed an honor guard on either side of Louis. The three ran together to the finish line.

The Greek victory in the race etched into the very culture of the nation, dissolved all the ill will of the previous seven days. Greeks hugged and kissed one another, they laughed and cried in an outpouring of emotion. Then they went looking for any foreigner, so they could let it be known that all the unhappiness was forgotten.

With a Greek the winner in the marathon, the Greek newspapers took a new position. The pride of Greece had been restored; now there were glowing reports of the magnificence of the First Olympiad of the modern era and how Greece and the rest of the world should immediately make plans for the next Olympiad four years hence.

The Olympic Games had passed their first hurdle, and a Greek shepherd, Spiridon Louis, was responsible for it when he traversed the historic distance from Marathon to Athens. And as Louis entered the stadium, more than one Greek patriot wept as he screamed: "Ne nikhkamen—Yes, we are victorious."

12. Marathon Madness

WHEN THE CHUBBY, UNATHLETIC YOUNG MAN chugged into Munich's Olympic stadium, the apparent winner of the grueling marathon run, 80,000 spectators roared in amazement. The scoreboard, which showed the progress of the runners, had just informed the packed audience that Frank Shorter of the United States was leading at the 40-kilometer mark by more than two minutes. At this stage, with less than two miles to go to the finish line, only a major catastrophe could prevent Shorter from winning the gold medal.

As the spectators scanned the program in an attempt to find out who had passed Shorter, there was frantic activity on the track. Officials and policemen were chasing the unknown lead runner, trying to move him off the track. Within a few moments, it became obvious that the malady known as "marathon madness" had once again climaxed the most historic and torturous event of the Olympic Games.

The hoax perpetrated by the young German was another in the seemingly unending string of strange events that has dominated the marathon since it was introduced at the first modern revival of the Olympics in 1896.

When two Greek princes jumped onto the track in Athens in 1896 to lead their victorious countryman, Spiridon Louis, across the finish line in the first marathon run, "marathon madness" had its opening act. Eight years later, at the St. Louis Games of 1904, a young American named Fred Lorz

Thirty-five-year-old Albin Stenroos crosses the finish line after winning the 1924 Paris Olympic marathon. Years earlier, Stenroos had broken his leg in competition and it was believed he was through with running.

was the first man across the finish line. As he was about to receive his gold medal from Alice Roosevelt, Olympic officials came running to the presentation stand. Within a few minutes, Lorz was unceremoniously shepherded out of the stadium, and British-born Tom Hicks, competing for the United States, was awarded the gold medal.

It seems that Lorz, suffering from leg cramps after nine miles, had hopped into a truck and traveled the next twelve miles sitting on the floor alongside the driver, out of sight. Then, six miles from the finish line and fully recuperated, Lorz had hopped out and continued the race. Besides losing the gold medal, Lorz was suspended from international competition for one year.

While the gold-medal shenanigans concerning Fred Lorz were taking place in the stadium, a more Olympian story was unfolding along the marathon route. Plodding along, an infectious smile on his face and a few words to spectators along the way, was Felix Carvajal, a postman from Cuba. A few months before the St. Louis games, Carvajal had a dream that he was destined to win the marathon. Many athletes have had similar dreams, but Carvajal's dream was more unusual. He had never run a competitive race in his life. Nevertheless, Carvajal set about getting financing for the St. Louis trip.

He began running around public squares in Havana to attract crowds. When enough people gathered, he would make speeches to the effect that he was going to win the gold medal in the St. Louis Olympics. He became a daily attraction in Havana and the butt of cruel jokes. More out of sympathy than interest, spectators would toss coins to him. His personal Olympic fund grew. Finally, he had enough money to make the trip to the United States.

When he got to New Orleans, he was robbed of all his money. He then began hitchhiking to St. Louis. When Carvajal arrived, he was greeted like a conquering hero. Fellow athletes began feeding the half-starved Cuban postman.

When the runners lined up for the marathon, Carvajal stood behind the starting line, looking like a performer from a traveling show. He was wearing heavy walking shoes, a long-sleeved shirt, and long trousers. To silence the laughter, one of the starters took scissors and snipped off Carvajal's trousers at the knees, at least giving the appearance that he was wearing shorts. A few more snips of the scissors, and his shirt became short-sleeved. There was nothing to be done about his heavy walking shoes, so the race began with Carvajal weighted down from the beginning.

Throughout the race, Carvajal kept up a steady stream of chatter with the other runners in the race and was amazed that the older, more experienced marathon runners were dropping out one by one.

Carvajal did not win, but, amazingly, he finished fourth. After the race, experts concluded that Carvajal, with proper training and proper shoes, could have won the Saint Louis marathon gold medal.

Prince George of Greece, all 6 feet 5 inches of him, gave a repeat performance of his 1896 final-lap run with the winner when he paced George Sherring of Canada across the finish line in the "unofficial" 1906 Games, again held in Athens. Prince George had the enviable record of twice crossing the finish line with the winner of the Marathon run.

The Paris marathon of 1924 was won by Albin Stenroos of Finland, perhaps the most unlikely candidate ever to win a gold medal. Stenroos started his athletic career as a wrestler but soon turned to running. In 1912 he finished third in the 10,000-meter run; soon after, he broke his leg while running in a cross-country race. His career appeared to be over.

He was unable to make the Finnish Olympic team competing at the 1920 Antwerp Games, but at age thirty-five, he decided to give it another try in Paris, four years later. Stenroos knew he had no chance in the 5,000- and 10,000-meter events dominated by his teammates, Paavo Nurmi and Villie Ritola, so he tried the marathon. At the finish line, Stenroos' margin of victory was one of the greatest in the history of the games—six minutes.

Kitei Son of Japan is listed in the record books as the winner of the 1936 Berlin marathon. Thirty-five years after his victory, it was revealed that he was from Korea. This fact is one indication of the high esteem in which the marathon race is held throughout the world. To the Japanese, the marathon is a revered race. To ensure a victory, the Japanese "recruited" Kitei Son, who was a student at a Japanese University. Fearing that his family would suffer reprisals if he made his Korean citizenship known, Kitei Son kept silent until 1971. Right before the Munich Games in 1972, the story came out.

After World War II, the Olympic Games were revived in London in 1948. A twenty-one-year-old paratrooper from Belgium, Étienne Gailly, made a promise to his friends that if he was able to finish the marathon, he would win a medal.

Gailly had never run the marathon before. He had competed in only cross-country races, less than half the distance of the 26-mile, 385-yard marathon run. He took the lead at the

157

Kitei Son, wearing a Japanese uniform, wins the 1936
marathon at the Berlin Olympics. More than thirty-five years
later, Kitei announced that he was actually from Korea.

Etienne Gailly of Belgium crosses the finish line to win the bronze medal at the 1948 London Olympics. Gailly was first into the stadium and only had to circle the track once for the gold medal. But Delfo Cabrera of Argentina and Tom Richards of Great Britain both passed him. Gailly collapsed at the finish line and was carried off the field on a stretcher.

10-kilometer mark and was running strongly. When he passed the 30-kilometer mark, still in the lead, it was the farthest he had ever run. By 40 kilometers, Delfo Cabrera of Argentina and Tom Richards made a challenge. They were within a few meters of each other.

Gailly entered the stadium first, but he was groggy. He was walking rather than running. He had only 400 meters to go to win the gold medal, but he was exhausted. Only courage kept him going.

Within 15 meters of Gailly, entering the stadium, was Cabrera. He passed Gailly. A few seconds later, Tom Richards entered the stadium. He, too, passed the reeling Gailly. Both Cabrera and Richards were running strongly, but Gailly was moving in slow motion.

Finally, Gailly stopped. He seemed as if he would topple onto the track. Meanwhile, Cabrera and Richards had crossed the finish line to win the gold and silver medals. As he stood motionless, the crowd was frantic, urging him on. They heralded Coleman of South Africa into the stadium. Gailly, with third place in jeopardy, began tottering to the finish line.

The scene was an incredible one. Gailly moving in slow motion, dragging one foot after another, staggered on as Coleman cut down the distance between them.

Finally, Gailly reached the finish line. Immediately he collapsed and was taken from the field on a stretcher. For a few hours there was fear for his life. Gailly was unable to attend the victory ceremony to receive his bronze medal, but it was given to him the following day. Étienne Gailly had fulfilled the promise he made to himself. He was still standing at the finish line, and he had won a medal.

Marathon fever hit the great Czechoslovakian champion Emil Zatopek at the 1952 Helsinki Games. After winning gold medals in the 10,000- and 5,000-meter races, he decided to try the marathon, a race he had never run before. In the middle of the race, he ran up to Jim Peters of Great Britain, the prerace favorite and one of the finest marathon runners in the world, who was setting a blistering pace.

Zatopek was laboring as he asked Peters, "Jim, is not the pace too fast?"

Trying to psych out the Czech, champion Peters replied, "Too fast? No, the pace is too slow."

A little perplexed, Zatopek nevertheless tore off, leaving Peters behind. One hour later, Zatopek crossed the finish line to win his third gold medal.

Winners of the Tokyo Olympic marathon in 1964. Ben
Heatley of Great Britain, second (left); Abebe Bikila,
Ethiopia, first (middle); and Kokichi Tsuburaya, Japan, third.
Tsuburaya pledged that he would avenge his 1964 loss by
winning the Mexico City marathon but he failed to make
the team. Eight months before the 1968 games, Tsuburaya,
depressed and despondent, committed suicide.

Of all the strange happenings during the running of the Olympic marathon, the most tragic took place following the Tokyo Games of 1964. Abebe Bikila won the race easily, but the battle for second place was between Kokichi Tsuburaya of Japan and Ben Heatley of Great Britain. They were within a few meters of each other as they approached the stadium.

Tsuburaya entered the stadium first. When the Japanese crowd saw their countryman move around the track, a loud roar resounded through the stadium. Coming in second to the incomparable Abebe Bikila was tantamount to victory. As Tsuburaya made his way down the track for the final 400 meters, Heatley entered the stadium, running strongly. Within a few meters, he passed the nearly exhausted Tsuburaya and sprinted to the finish line the winner of the silver medal. Tsuburaya staggered to a third-place finish.

In the days that followed, Tsuburaya brooded. The humiliation of being passed by Heatley in front of the emperor and 80,000 of his countrymen was too much for him to bear. In the following three years, Tsuburaya began to train in the hope that he would redeem himself at the 1968 Mexico City Olympics. On January 9, 1968, Kokichi Tsuburaya committed suicide. A note next to his body read, "I cannot run anymore."

13. Man O'War Loses in an "Upset"

MAN O'WAR WAS VOTED THE GREATEST THOR-oughbred of the half century, the period between 1900 and 1950. If a poll were taken today, Man o'War's position would most probably move down a few notches—behind Secretariat and perhaps Citation, the Triple Crown winner of 1948 who went on to become a millionaire after the half-century poll was concluded.

Comparisons of Man o'War with later great thoroughbreds have the same futile conclusions that result in the never-ending arguments that compare Jack Dempsey and Muhammed Ali, Bill Tilden and Rod Laver, or Bobby Jones and Jack Nicklaus.

Man o'War was the superhorse in the years 1919–20. In his first race as a two-year-old, he was sent off as a 3–5 favorite. In all his subsequent races, he was never less than a 7–10 choice. Three times during his two-year career, a bettor had to risk $100 to win a single buck. Man o'War ended his career with purses totaling $249,465. Adjusted to today's finances, that figure places him well past the millionaire status. "Big Red" was the golden name in horse racing in the golden age of sports. Every time he ran, he took the headlines away from Babe Ruth, Jack Dempsey, and Ty Cobb. He won twenty out of twenty-one starts. His record would have been unblemished if not for bad racing luck in his seventh start as a two-year-old.

163

The only known photograph of Man o'War's lone defeat. In two years of racing, Man o'War won twenty out of twenty-one starts. Johnny Loftus, the only jockey to ride Man o'War in 1919, is in the saddle. A few yards from the finish line, Man o'War trails Upset.

The Sanford Memorial Stakes held on August 13, 1919, was the highlight event for two-year-olds at the Saratoga Race Track summer meeting. It was a six-furlong race. Man o'War and the second favorite, Golden Broom, were assigned the top weights of 130 pounds.

The morning of the race, Mars Cassidy, a starter with the reputation of being the finest ever, called in sick. He was replaced by C. H. Pettingill, a finish-line judge with little experience.

At the starting line, Man o'War was assigned the next-to-outside post position in the field of seven. In his previous six races, "Big Red" had gained the reputation as a notoriously fractious starter, usually rearing up on his hind legs and giving his jockey fits. Jockey Johnny Loftus was up on Man o'War. As "Big Red" neared the starting line, Loftus was having trouble straightening him out.

Starting races in 1919 was primitive compared to today's individual gate stalls. Then, a restraining roped barrier was stretched across the width of the track with the horses lined up as best as possible behind it. The official starter would wait for the moment when the horses were in equal alignment. All too often, a nervous thoroughbred would break the barrier in advance of the starter's call. The race would have to be restarted. Under the prevailing conditions, it was nearly impossible for the field to get off in a perfect start.

164

Man o'War poses in the classic thoroughbred stance. He lived thirty years and, after his retirement as a three-year-old, he was Kentucky's major tourist attraction at owner Sam Riddle's farm.

Trying to beat Man o'War out, Golden Broom broke the barrier three times. The third favorite, Upset, carrying only 115 pounds, broke twice.

Finally, starter Pettingill sent them off. Six of the seven thoroughbreds got off reasonably well with Golden Broom dashing for the rail and the lead. The seventh, Man o'War, was practically left at the post. The field had gone four lengths before "Big Red" took his first stride forward.

At the first turn, Golden Broom, running easily, was in the lead, followed by Upset. Man o'War, recovering quickly from the poor start, settled into the pace, and soon his magnificent twenty-four-foot stride began cutting down the distance between him and the leaders.

As they came off the turn for the stretch run, Golden Broom suddenly quit. Upset passed him halfway down the stretch. Man o'War, now flying, also passed Golden Broom and started after Upset. There was no question that "Big Red" was now moving fast. It was only a matter of whether the stretch would run out before he caught Upset.

A hundred yards from the finish, Man o'War was a length and a half in back of Upset. At the wire, Upset was still a half length in front. Man o'War had lost his first race.

Man o'War went on to win his next three starts as a two-year-old, compiling a record of nine victories in ten starts. The following year, 1920, the jockey weights assigned to him became more monstrous with each race. Owner Sam Riddle decided to keep him out of the Kentucky Derby because he felt that no horse should carry 126 pounds over the ten-furlong distance so early in the racing season. Later, Man o'War won the Preakness and Belmont Stakes. He finished as a three-year-old with a perfect record—eleven straight victories. Man o'War was then retired.

Said Riddle, "If he ran any more, handicappers would have assigned weights to him that would force him to break down. He had done enough. He deserved to stay healthy and live out his life."

Sam Riddle was correct. Man o'War lived to the age of thirty, the equivalent of 105 human years.

14.
The One-in-a-Million Shot

CHANDLER HARPER WALKED TO THE 18TH GREEN ON the final day of the 1953 Tam O'Shanter golf tournament acknowledging the cheers of the crowd. He had just made an incredible second shot on the par-4, 410-yard final hole. His ball rested just two feet from the cup. Calmly, Harper holed the putt for a birdie 3, giving him a four-day total of 279 and a one-stroke lead over Lew Worsham, who was playing directly behind him and waiting to tee off on the final hole.

Harper's birdie was a defiant response to the charge of Worsham, who had electrified the crowd with a dramatic seven-foot birdie putt on the 17th hole to place him in a temporary tie with Harper. With one hole to play, Worsham had finally gotten even with Harper, who started the final 18 holes with a one stroke advantage.

Worsham heard the cheers after Harper sank his final birdie putt, and by the roar of the crowd he knew he was in trouble. He would have to duplicate Harper's birdie to send the match into a sudden death playoff.

To this point, Worsham had had an up-and-down tourney. He had shot a tremendous 65 on opening day, to lead the field by three strokes. Then he fell back with a 72 and 73 on the second and third days, to trail Harper and Al Besselink by one stroke as the final eighteen holes got under way.

Photo sequence shows Lou Worsham 140 yards from the hole taking his second shot on the par-4 18th. The ball clears a small stone fence and bounces into the cup.

With Harper's round finished, Worsham teed off and hit a magnificent 270-yard drive down the fairway. He still had a formidable crowd with him, and they gathered around as he took a wedge out for his second shot. From approximately the same position, minutes before, Harper had placed his second shot two feet from the cup to set up his birdie 3 for the lead.

Worsham's tee shot was very similar to Harper's. He had a clear shot to a green that was protected by a two-foot-high stone barrier. Between the stone barrier and the green was a ten-foot-wide creek.

Worsham would have to make certain, as Harper did, that his wedge was enough club to clear the barrier and make the

green. If he was short of the stone barrier, or if he hit the creek, his chance for a tie was over. The ideal shot would be a duplicate of Harper's—loft to the green and pray for a good roll.

For Worsham, the 1947 National Open champion, the precarious situation was the same one he had faced at the Tam O'Shanter the year before. Then, leading with nine holes to play, he had blown sky high on the back nine and had lost the tournament.

From his position 140 yards away, Worsham could see the pin. He was surrounded by a sizable crowd that flanked his left and right sides. Worsham stood over the ball exactly nine

169

seconds. Immediately after he made contact, the crowd on both sides of him broke ranks. Some ran toward the green, to get an advantageous position for the final moments. The majority moved toward Worsham as the ball was still in flight. They would make the walk with him to the green.

The ball bounced softly on the green, took a second shorter bounce, then a third about four feet from the pin. Then slowly, agonizingly, it rolled to the flag and disappeared. The ball had gone in.

The films show a man on the green waving his right arm wildly.

In the distance, fans began jumping up and down. It is not certain whether they knew that Worsham's shot had gone in or whether they thought he had put it close enough for a birdie attempt. Almost immediately, the cheers and the jumping up and down of excited spectators told those surrounding Worsham that the miracle had truly taken place.

Worsham began the long walk to the pin to confirm what he already knew. The incredible 140-yard wedge shot had given him an eagle 2 for a 1-stroke victory over Chandler Harper. The eagle gave Worsham a final-day total of 68, two strokes better than Harper's 70. Harper led by one stroke as the final day's play began.

The dramatic finish had no precedent in championship golf history. The closest to it was the historic double-eagle spoon shot by Gene Sarazan on the 15th hole of the final day of the Masters in 1935. Sarazan had holed his second shot on the par-5 15th to pick up three strokes and tie him for the lead with Craig Wood. Sarazan went on to win the Masters in a playoff.

This incredible shot won Worsham the $15,000 first prize. Harper's second-place money was $10,000.

PERHAPS THE FINEST HOURS IN THE HISTORY OF THE Navy football team took place on November 30, 1946, when the Middies lost a 21–18 thriller to the powerhouse cadets of Army led by the incomparable backfield trio of Glenn Davis, Doc Blanchard, and Arnold Tucker. Thousands of words were written in the postgame tribute to the Middies who, after losing eight straight games during the season, played Army to a standstill—just missing a dramatic upset victory as the clock ran out with the ball a few yards short of the goal line.

Now, these many years later, "instant replay" of the game films placed in synchronization with the actual radio broadcast of the game unfolds a series of boners by the Middies in the last eighty seconds that prevented them from pulling off the upset of the century.

The 1946 Army football team was perhaps the most popular in modern football history. Their exploits on the football field during the 1944–46 seasons had taken them through twenty-seven games without a loss.

It was the era when Army vs. Navy was The Game, the climax to every football season. The wartime service-academy football teams held a special symbolic significance to a then united country; the young men competing on the gridiron were the future MacArthur's and Eisenhower's for the Army, and the Halsey's and Nimitz's for the Navy. This, too, was the era before the platoon system. Players with the powerful

171

offensive reputation of Davis and Blanchard performed equally well on defense and were often times iron men, playing the entire sixty minutes of the game.

Army was a 28-point favorite. Earlier in the season the Cadets and Notre Dame had battled to a scoreless tie in what was then termed as the game that would decide the national championship. As it turned out, Notre Dame was named the nation's top team at the end of the year—probably because of Navy's dramatic effort, which fell just short of victory.

Army was ranked number one in the nation in both 1944 and 1945, and a convincing victory over Navy in 1946 would probably have earned them that spot for the third straight year. It was not to be. Navy's great game dissipated the Army mystique, and Notre Dame was voted the nation's top team.

Navy had won its opening game and then had proceeded to lose eight in a row. Ironically, the Middies had given Army its last defeat before the 27-game streak began—on the last day of the 1943 season when they upended the Cadets 13–0. In 1944 Army won 23–7, and the following year they all but humiliated the Midshipmen with a 32–13 romp.

Only the Midshipmen themselves thought they had a chance in 1946 as the 103,000 fans settled in their seats for the opening kickoff. President Harry Truman and his wife, Bess, were seated on the Navy side during the first half, but their presence brought the Navy little luck.

Arnold Tucker and Glenn Davis combined for the first Army score with Davis taking a pitchout from his quarterback and outracing the Navy secondary for 13 yards and the score. Jack Ray's extra point made it 7–0. Navy came roaring back as quarterback Reeves Baysinger climaxed an 82-yard drive by plunging over from the 1-yard line. The extra point was missed, and Navy trailed 7–6.

With this their last college game, the Blanchard-Davis combination picked the second quarter to put on their last great performances. Blanchard went 52 yards for the second Cadet score, and Ray's extra point made it 14–6. A few minutes later Davis showed his versatility on three successive plays. From the Navy 38, Davis passed 8 yards to Poole, then took the ball himself for another 4 yards. Then Davis passed to Blanchard in the left flank; Doc took it 26 yards into the end zone. Ray's third straight extra point made it 21–6, and the rout seemed under way.

Halftime arrived without further scoring, and President Truman made the traditional walk across the field to the Army side in what turned out later to be an ironic omen.

Pete Williams and Tom Hawkins of Navy (both on extreme left) await the snap from center on the final play of the game.

Hawkins faking a buck into the line tosses a lateral to Williams, who starts to his right.

Army started out the second half as they ended the first, but two questionable calls by the usually impeccable Arnold Tucker turned the game around. Army took the kickoff and drive down to the Navy 31-yard line where they had fourth down and 2 yards to go for a first down. Mysteriously, Tucker decided to punt, and when Davis kicked out of bounds on the Navy 22, even the Middies were perplexed.

This Army miscalculation gave Navy new life. They drove 78 yards for their second touchdown with Pete Williams, Bill Hawkins, and Al McCully tearing holes in the vaunted Army line all the way down to the goal. The extra point was again missed, and Navy trailed 21–12.

Army took the ensuing kickoff, but now Tucker came up with another strange call. The Cadets had first down on their own 25-yard line. In three plays they were inches short of their 35 and a first down. Where Tucker had played it safe in Navy territory a few moments before, he now took a suicidal gamble in his own back yard. Army would try for the first down.

Tucker gave the job to Blanchard, who tried to muscle through the Navy center but was met head on by All-American Dick Scott for no gain. Navy took over on the Army 34. In two sequences Tucker's play calling had put Navy back in the ball game.

Navy moved to the 5-yard line as the third period ended, and on the second play of the final period Bill Earl tossed 2 yards to Captain Leon Bramlett in the end zone for the third Navy touchdown. The extra point was again missed, but now Navy had completely taken the momentum away from the Cadets. And there were still fourteen minutes left in the game.

Neither team could sustain a drive as the fourth period wore on. When the Middies returned a Blanchard kick to their own 33 with a little more than four minutes to play, there was nothing to indicate they were going to have any more luck. But they pecked and clawed their way to the Army 23-yard line. With fourth down and 2 yards to go for a first down, fullback Lynn Chewning took off on a mad dash to the Army 3-yard line before Tucker and Davis combined to make a saving tackle. (Both Blanchard and Davis played the entire game, and Arnold Tucker was in for all but two minutes.) Now Navy had first down with 3 yards to go for a touchdown *with ninety seconds to go in the game.* (There is conflict as to the exact amount of time remaining in the game. All the newspaper accounts report that there were ninety seconds to play in the game when Chewning was tackled at the 3-yard line. In re-

Williams at the 11-yard line tries to skirt the right end.

Williams sees the Army defenders blocking his path. He could have run out of bounds, stopping the clock for one more play. However, he plants his right foot to turn inside toward the playing field.

Williams is now committed to his decision to try to score. He's at the 8-yard line but there are Army defenders on either side and in front of him.

At the 6-yard line, Williams is hit from all sides by Army players.

Williams goes down in a pile of Cadets.

Williams looks to the sidelines fearing the worst. He is not out of bounds and there is no more time left. Final score: Army, 21; Navy, 18.

listening to Harry Wismer's play-by-play account of the game, he *four* times mentions that *there were eighty seconds to play.*)

The time left to play proved crucial in more than one area, according to Coach Tom Hamilton of Navy when we spoke recently—some thirty years after the action. Recalled Hamilton: "The stadium was in an uproar and fans broke from the stands and converged on the sidelines—some of them moving on to the playing field. The noise was incredible and the place was a bedlam. President Truman had left the stadium a few minutes before Chewning's run, and many of the guards and security people left their sideline posts to help in escorting him from the stadium."

The time left to play, President Truman's leaving the stadium, and the fans' converging on the field all joined together in making contact between Coach Hamilton and quarterback Baysinger impossible. Baysinger was left on his own as Hamilton frantically tried to signal him.

The clock was running as Baysinger again called Chewning to carry the ball on first down. He was stopped cold at the line of scrimmage by a charged-up Army line.

"I can't criticize Baysinger these many years later," said Coach Hamilton. "He's dead and can't reply to anything I might say. Reeves played such a magnificent game to get us to that point that I don't want to criticize him. However, if I was able to contact him I would have called different plays on first and second downs. It was essential that *we stop the clock.* We either had to run to the sidelines to get out of bounds or pass into the end zone. A touchdown of course would have won it, and an incomplete pass would have stopped the clock. I definitely did not like the selection of plays at that point."

The clock was still running, with less than a minute to play, when Baysinger again called Chewning's number. The powerful substitute fullback again threw himself into the Army line, and again the Cadets, led by All-American Hank Foldberg, held. The ball was still at the 3-yard line, and the clock was still running.

"It was here that *I blew the game.* I called for a time out knowing that we were going to be penalized five yards for excessive time outs. I made the decision because I was scared we wouldn't get another play off. At that moment I thought I had no choice. I preferred having the ball on the eight-yard line with the chance of two more cracks at the touchdown than having the possibility of the clock running out without getting off another play," Hamilton recalled sadly.

Coach Hamilton sent in Pete Williams. The ball was on the 8-yard line now, and Williams came in with the play from the bench. It was to be a buck lateral.

Hawkins took a direct pass from center, started to the center, then tossed to Williams on his right. Williams tried desperately to skirt the Army left side but picked up only 3 yards, to the 5-yard line, before he was slammed down.

In reviewing this final play of the game in "instant replay" frame by frame, it becomes apparent that Pete Williams also found the spectators at the sidelines intimidating. He moved to his right and could have made it out of bounds to give Navy one final play. However, he chose to cut in from the sidelines to try to bull his way through Army defenders for the final yards. The spectators were on the verge of complete pandemonium. The clock was running, people were surrounding the field, and the two teams were trying to regroup for another play. The gun sounded, and the game was over.

"Again, not wishing to be overly critical," Coach Hamilton recounted, "I think the referee would not have been out of order in ruling that Williams *had gone out of bounds* even though he technically did not reach the sidelines. *There were no sidelines anymore.* So many people had come on the field that there was no way of telling where the sidelines were. Williams had very little running room."

Coach Hamilton appears to be wrong when he states that spectators had come onto the field. A careful look at the game films does show thousands of fans standing at the sidelines—*but not on* the playing field. Nevertheless this seemingly solid wall of people on the sidelines could have affected Baysinger's thinking in not running in that direction on the first two downs.

The films add credibility to this theory. The last three plays all began at the inbounds marker, only 15 to 20 yards from the sidelines, which would have made it easy for Navy to run out of bounds to stop the clock. The mass of spectators might have deterred Baysinger from that attempt.

It might seem unfair to fault Navy after they performed so gallantly. However, the game clearly shows that the Army defenses were geared for straight-ahead thrusts by the Navy. There is no question that Navy lost the game because they couldn't stop the clock.

Countless words were written about Navy's courageous performance, but strangely enough, not one of the postgame stories mentioned that in reality Navy could put the ball into play *only three times* in the last eighty seconds. When Chewning was stopped on first down for no gain, there was no play possible other than an end-zone pass or a run out of bounds to stop the clock. It was Baysinger's call of a running play on second down that probably lost the ball game for Navy.

Nevertheless, everyone went home happy. Army, because it maintained its three-year winning streak and Navy because it came so close after being a 28-point underdog.

16.
"Miss Poker Face" Takes a Walk

"MISS POKER FACE" VS. THE "ICE DOLLY" WOULD have been perhaps the most dramatic confrontation in the history of Forest Hills or Wimbledon women's tennis. Helen Wills Moody was queen of the courts in the 1920s and early 1930s. Chris Evert holds the same position four decades later, but no tennis champions in the interim were as similar in ice-cold, unflappable court demeanor as these two.

As cool as Chris Evert is, those who have seen both players claim that Chris is a bundle of nerves compared to sphinxlike Helen Wills Moody. In her reign as undisputed champion of women's tennis from 1922 to 1931, no one remembers Helen Wills Moody ever making a negative gesture at a missed shot, or glaring at a linesman over a bad call, or saying a word to an opponent throughout a match.

Helen Wills Moody was all business. She walked onto the court to play, and that's all she did. It is doubtful that the histrionics and sometimes hysterical shenanigans of today's players would have earned from her even the slightest smile or frown. Queen Helen most probably would have patiently waited for the furor to subside and then methodically smashed her opponent off the court.

On August 27, 1933, twenty-eight-year-old Helen Wills Moody stepped onto the center court of Forest Hills to meet her long-time rival, Helen Jacobs, in the final of the United States Women's Championship. To most, the result was a foregone conclusion.

Helen Wills Moody (left) and Helen Jacobs, a few minutes
before they will step onto the court for their August 26, 1933,
controversial Forest Hills final.

Helen Jacobs had never won a set from Helen Wills Moody. In fact, Helen Wills Moody had not lost a single set in the Forest Hills championships since 1925. She brought to Forest Hills in 1933 eight Wimbledon championships and seven Forest Hills championships. She and Bill Tilden were the reigning queen and king of the world of tennis in the sports era known as the golden age. The motions of going through this final were considered a mere formality.

There was some apprehension among Queen Helen's entourage when she lost the first set to Helen Jacobs 8–6. This was only the third set she had lost in competition over a six-year period. "Little Miss Poker Face" evened matters with a 6–3 victory in the second set. Now the jam-packed crowd at Forest Hills waited for the queen to chop down her long-time challenger methodically in the third set.

Helen Jacobs broke Helen Wills Moody's service in the first game and held her own, for a 2–0 lead. Jacobs broke Moody again, and the score became 3–0.

At this point the most controversial moment in the history of the Forest Hills championships took place. As the two women were changing courts, Helen Wills Moody put on her sweater, walked to the referee's chair, and told him that she could not continue. Without a word to Helen Jacobs, Helen Wills Moody walked off the court.

The crowd could not believe it. Even though there was precedent for such action—twelve years before, the then reigning queen, Suzanne Lenglen of France, had defaulted to Molla Mallory early in the second set of their second-round match—nobody could conceive that a player could walk off during the U.S. Championship final.

The press did not take kindly to Moody's walkout. She was labeled, at best, a poor sport; at worst she was called an "outright quitter."

In the locker room Helen Wills Moody made the following statement: "In the third set of my singles match I felt as if I was going to faint because of the pain in my back and hip and a complete numbness of my right leg. The match was long and by defaulting, I do not wish to detract from the excellence of Miss Jacobs' play. I feel that I have spoiled the finish of the national championship and wish that I had followed the advice of my doctor and returned to California. I still feel that I did right in withdrawing because I felt that I was on the verge of collapse on the court."

The mention of her doctor's advice was, to many, an additional piece of arrogance designed to demean Helen Jacobs' victory. Those close to the tennis scene, however, were aware that Moody had injured her back while lifting some heavy rocks. She was under a doctor's care when she competed at Wimbledon, and despite severe pain, she was able to win the coveted English Championship. But she had made no mention of her injury before the opening round of Forest Hills play.

Helen Wills Moody put her own end to the story in her autobiography when she wrote: "My choice was instinctive rather than premeditated. Had I been able to think clearly, I might have chosen to remain. Animals and human beings, however, prefer to suffer in a quiet dark place."

Helen Wills Moody's reputation suffered greatly because of the Forest Hills incident. If she had gone through the motions during the last three games of the third set, even in defeat she would have remained the incomparable champion. The unflappable Queen Helen had to realize that championships must always be won and lost in the arena.

Helen Wills Moody (in the far court) gets ready to backhand her return to Helen Jacobs in the third set of their match.

183

Trailing 0–3 in the third and final set of their
championship match, Helen Wills Moody walks off the
court and defaults to Helen Jacobs.

Moody has just told the umpire that she can no longer continue.
Jacobs has been informed that the championship is hers.

Helen Wills Moody and Helen Jacobs leave the court.

Helen Jacobs receives the championship trophy,
the Holcombe Ward Cup.

17.
What's in the Future for Instant Replay?

THERE ARE FEW OBJECTIVE SPORTS FANS. TO MOST of them, officials are good or bad depending upon the outcome of a controversial decision.

The fan is fickle, constantly changing and rechanging his opinion of an official depending upon the fortunes of his favorite team. To those who bet, decisions costing them money create responses that sometimes question the honesty of the official.

Should officials use mechanical assistance in judging plays? Perhaps the most vocal opponent of mechanical assistance has been Pete Rozelle, commissioner of the National Football League. Rozelle repeatedly cites the obvious negatives associated with the use of such aids: the games would be lengthened and boredom would result if instant replay were called upon to settle every coach's beef; different camera angles often give the same play different interpretations; and the cost of camera equipment would discourage many club owners from installing it. This last objection probably would be the easiest to overcome—if installation of such equipment could give definitive answers to 100 percent of the controversies.

In sports such as horse racing, film and photographs are the final means used to determine riding infractions and finish-line decisions. But film is suitable to horse racing because these controversies are decided *after* the event is completed. In sports such as football, basketball, boxing, baseball, tennis, and ice hockey, controversies are always occurring and must be ruled upon while the game is in progress. This alone makes the delay of play impractical and, even more, unfair.

Perhaps the most important ingredient in the outcome of any contest after talent and luck are considered is endurance—the condition of the athlete. Many a victory has been snatched from defeat because of conditioning—the athlete's ability to sustain top-flight performance throughout an *entire* contest.

Every sport has its legal times-out. Boxing has its one-minute interval between rounds, football and basketball have play interruptions prescribed in their rules, and tennis has rest periods after every odd-numbered game. Rest periods are as important a part of the game's final outcome as talent and coaching.

Consider the running back recouping his energies while officials meditate over instant replay, the tennis player renewing her strength while play is stopped, the basketball player receiving a five-minute "free" time-out when he is all but exhausted. These breaks in play change the structure of the games and give advantages where none was intended.

Instant replay and slow motion are able to dissect controversial plays moments after they occur. With television and TV viewers becoming more sophisticated each year, the home viewer has become a juryman rather than just a spectator. Officials have been spared the abuse of many millions because the vocal response hurled against them has been confined to the home. This, however, may be changing. More and more stadium managements are debating the idea of placing giant screens inside the stadium so that the 80,000 or so fans in attendance have the same luxury as the stay-at-homes to vent their fury at the hapless officials. The dedicated official has had, up until now, enough trouble without having to face this additional burden from week to week.

The argument that modern technology can give instant re-viewing to an official and thus help him to solve all problems has little validity. Any curtailment of play because of new technology, even that limited to less than a minute, presents many new problems.

The photo finish has revolutionized decision making when called upon to decide a race. But during the course of a contest, as Commissioner Rozelle points out, "officials make approximately 29,000 calls a season." The calls that raise controversy are few—a minuscule percentage. Until technology is advanced to the point where it can assist the official 100 percent of the time, instantaneously, during the controversial moments of a game, there is no room for instant replay.

For every obvious wrong call of an official that is detected by "instant replay," there is an equal amount of controversy that is out of the range of the cameras or that can be distorted by the placement of cameras and the nature of video.

Athletes are human. So are officials. If we cannot expect perfection from the performers, how can we expect more from those who officiate? The structure of sport is based on the premise that all one can ask of an athlete is that he or she be dedicated, prepared, talented and courageous. Can anyone doubt that these qualifications do not hold true for officials?

Index